GRACE

*God's Divine Influence
Upon Our
Heart
And
His Expression
In and Through
Our Life*

Carolyn Ann Bardsley

**GRACE: God's Divine Influence Upon Our Heart
And His Expression In and Through Our Life**

Copyright © 2016 by Carolyn Ann Bardsley

All Rights Reserved

Unless otherwise noted, the Scripture quotations contained herein are from the *Revised Standard Version of the Bible,* copyright 1946, 1952, 1971 by the Division of Christian Education of the National Council of Churches of Christ in the USA. Used by permission.

ISBN-13: 978-1536944976

ISBN-10: 1536944971

Contents

Preface i
Chapter 1: Grace Defined 1
   Unmerited Favor—An Impoverished Interpretation 1
   A More Accurate Interpretation of Grace 5
   Living In Grace Is Not Optional 7
   A Grace That Saves—My Experience 10
   Grace Is God's Spirit Working In and Through Us 12
   Grace Is a Gift That Must Be Received and Lived 13
   Grace and Faith Versus Law and Works 16
   Living In Grace Is Faith 20

Chapter 2: Divine Influence—God Reigning In Us 23
   Reconciliation With God Our Father 23
   Grace Is a Matter of Life or Death 25
   To Live In Grace We Have to Lose Our Life 32
   Either God Reigns or Satan Is In Control 36
   Obedience from the Heart 39
   Repentance Is Not a One Time Event 41
   The Kingdom of God Is Within Us 46
   LORD Means God Is Reigning Within 48
   Jesus Made God Our Father LORD of His Life 52
   We Are the Temple of the Living God 54
   God Must Be Our Lord or We Are Still Under the Law 57

Chapter 3: Heart-Relationship With God 59
   Thoughts, Words, and Actions Originate In Our Heart 60
   The Redeemed Heart Is Where God's Spirit Resides 61
   The Redeemed Heart Is Where We Hear God's Voice 64
   The Heart Understands; The Mind Interprets 66
   We Believe With Our Heart, Not Our Mind 68
   The Heart Is Where We Obey God 72
   God Wants Willing Obedience, Not Dutiful Compliance 74
   God Wants a Personal Relationship With Us 79

    God Desires Love—A Function of Our Heart 83
    There Is No Other Definition for Love Than God Is Love .. 86
    God Designed Us to Live in Oneness With Him 88
    The Heart Is Deceitful When God Is Not Reigning Within 92
    Our Heart—Our Holy Of Holies 95

Chapter 4: God's Expression in Our Life 99
    God's Works—Not Our Own Good Works 99
    Living In Grace Is Doing God's Will 109
    God Speaks and We Hear and Obey His Voice 112
    God's Spirit In Us Teaches Us ALL Things 116
    God's Spirit Sanctifies and Purifies 119
    God Reigning In Us Keeps Us from Sinning 121
    We Love As God Loves 133
    We Bear Fruit—Fruits of God's Spirit In Us 139
    We Demonstrate God's Power—Gifts of God's Spirit 140

Chapter 5: Jesus Is Grace Manifested 145
    Jesus Is Our Role Model for Living In Grace 145
    Jesus Always Pointed Us to Father God 149
    We Are Conformed to the Image of God's Son 151
    Christ Set Us Free—Free from Law and Sin 157
    Grace Explains What It Means to Believe In Jesus 160
    Consequences of Not Living In Grace 163
    Sinning Against God's Spirit—The Unforgivable Sin 166
    Eternal Life Now—Knowing God and Jesus Christ 169
    Kingdom of God—Heaven 173
    Final Thoughts on Grace 175

Appendix: Grace—An Epistle Greeting and Ending 179

About the Author 187

Preface

I am writing this book about grace because I never want to forget what God showed me about the importance of grace and how central it is to my faith.

When you hear the word *grace*, doesn't it make you joyful to know you are under grace and not the law? We often sing about grace but do we really know what grace is and how to live in grace?

I saw a funny video on television the other day. A young boy was so excited Christmas morning that he could hardly wait to open his gifts. He excitedly rips open his first gift and starts dancing around as if he had his greatest desire fulfilled. Finally he looks at the gift more closely and asks with a puzzled look "What is it?" The audience finds it quite amusing.

Do we, as Christians, know what the gift of grace is? We can mentally receive God's gift of grace, but practically not enter into it because we don't really understand what it is.

I had interpreted *grace* to mean "God's unmerited favor" because the Amplified Bible interprets grace as "undeserved or unmerited favor." Pastors in their sermons have also defined grace as "unmerited favor." So to me grace was God giving me blessings I did not deserve and mercy was God not giving me punishment which I did deserve.

When I read *you are saved by grace and not by obeying the law*, I applied my interpretation of grace and mercy. Since Christ died for my sin, I am under grace. Therefore God blesses me with salvation even though I do not deserve it. Since I am not under the law, God does not punish me for not being able to fulfill the law.

Now I see that this interpretation fails to convey what the early disciples and writers of the Bible understood and intended to communicate when they used the word *grace*.

Like many Christians, I thought I knew what grace meant and had not questioned my understanding until recently when I was going through a hard time. I was reading in Corinthians when the following verse caught my attention:

> *My grace is sufficient for you, for my power is made perfect in weakness.*   2 Corinthians 12:9

When I applied my heretofore interpretation of grace as "God's unmerited favor," it did not encourage my soul.

I was weak and needed strength to overcome the testing of my faith. I was struggling and looking for encouragement. I was, as they say, in a teachable moment.

So on this day, I decided to find out why grace was so important to Paul and the early Christians and how it was supposed to help me now in my weakness.

In this book I want to record what I learned and why it has been so significant in my life. I also want to capture my excitement about this revelation so that if God should someday allow me to share this good news with another, I will be able to do so with the freshness and intensity that I feel today.

When I share my excitement about the richness of grace with other Christians, I notice that many are quite content to continue interpreting grace as God's unmerited favor. This alarms me because I know that in times of crisis or hardship having an accurate understanding of grace can mean the difference between having an enduring faith or becoming disappointed in God and losing faith. I see this book as a stake in the ground, which will help me persevere in times of testing of my faith.

This book contains the Scriptures on which I base my new understanding of grace. In my book *Living In Grace* I share my testimony of how I live in grace—*God's divine influence upon my heart and His expression in and through my life*.

I ask God to open the eyes of our heart to the inexpressible richness of grace.

Carolyn Bardsley
June 2016

Amazing Grace

Amazing grace! How sweet the sound—
That saved a wretch like me!
I once was lost but now am found.
Was blind but now I see

Through many dangers, toils, and snares,
I have already come;
Tis grace that brought me safe thus far,
And grace will lead me home

Chapter 1: Grace Defined

For a new believer, "believe God" may mean believing the words God spoke as recorded in the Bible. Later, as our faith matures, we learn to listen and obey God's voice as He speaks directly to us. We learn that believing God is not just mental agreement with words written long ago, but allowing God to live in and through us now.

Although both interpretations are correct, the first misses that God not only recorded words for us to read, but He also is a *LIVING* God who desires a love relationship by speaking directly with us today. The same is true for the word "grace."

Unmerited Favor—An Impoverished Interpretation

"Unmerited favor" is the common interpretation of grace widely used in sermons and Christian books. The Amplified Version of the Bible uses this definition and adds words such as "blessing, loving kindness, goodwill, and mercy." Grace interpreted as unmerited favor is accurate in the sense that God shows us unmerited favor by Jesus having paid for our sins on the cross. But unmerited favor is an *impoverished interpretation* of grace.

Grace interpreted as unmerited favor is a good beginning point for the new believer learning about his or her sinful nature and the need for God's mercy, but it is an incomplete interpretation for the more mature believer whom God asks to be led by His Spirit.

*If we **live by the Spirit**, let us also **walk by the Spirit**.*
Galatians 5:25

> *For all who are **led by the Spirit of God** are sons of God.*   Romans 8:14

When we interpret grace as God's favor and blessing, we focus on God's gifts rather than God Himself as the gift. God, in the form of the Holy Spirit in us, is the free gift of grace given to us. God is the blessing.

What troubles me most about interpreting grace as unmerited favor is that it makes God out to be a benevolent magistrate remote from us rather than an intimate Father who gives us His Spirit within. In reality, God desires to be one with us, not remote and separated from us.

With this interpretation of grace, I can see why believers become discouraged when tribulations and hard times come. If we think that grace means blessing, we expect blessing, not hardship. This can inadvertently lead believers on a perilous path of discouragement in hard times. And hard times will surely come to believers.

This unmerited-favor focus can lead Christians to falsely believe they are in good standing with God. Blessings, however, are to bring us to the LORD, not to make us falsely confident in our relationship with God.

> *Do you presume upon the riches of His kindness and forbearance and patience? Do you not know that God's kindness is meant to lead you to repentance?*
>   Romans 2:4

God blesses the unbeliever and believer alike with worldly goods, but only believers receive His presence in the form of the Holy Spirit. God gives gifts to all, but He gives everyone choice to receive His indwelling presence or not.

Grace is not about God-given presents but about God giving His presence.

When we use unmerited favor as the meaning of grace, I can see how we get into doing good works that the Bible frequently warns us against. Even though unmerited, we hope we can please God to get extra blessings. We do our good works to be in good standing with God. We give of ourselves because we obey Scriptures rather than from a heartfelt motivation given us by God's Spirit within. God asks for love, but we interpret that to mean working for Him. We obey Scriptures rather than the *Living* God within because we focus on gifts from God rather than God's gift of Himself.

Emphasizing the free gift nature of grace can lead us to falsely believe we have nothing to do to receive grace. Unmerited can imply that there is nothing we can or need to do to live in grace. Grace just is. When we become a Christian we just get this free gift of grace. If one thinks of grace as God's favor or blessing, then this is true. If, however, we realize that God is offering His presence to us, then it is another story. God does not force Himself on us. Love never forces itself upon another. We always retain the right to refuse. God, who is love, desires to live in and through us. He gives us choice to love Him or not—to give ourselves to Him or not. *This free gift of grace must be received and lived.*

Interpreting grace as unmerited favor implies we are still unworthy of relationship with God our Father. Unmerited suggests we are unworthy and it is just the graciousness of God to not wipe us out. This nullifies the work of Christ on the cross that restored our relationship with God our Father. He paid the price for our sins and tore down the curtain that separated us from the Holy of Holies. We are to enter with confidence as sons and daughters not as unworthy patrons.

If grace means God's unmerited favor, what did Peter mean when he said:

> ***Grow in the grace*** *and knowledge of our Lord and Savior Jesus Christ.* 2 Peter 3:18

How does one grow in God's unmerited favor?

Grace interpreted as unmerited favor fails to recognize our Living Savior and LORD and His work in our lives. This definition of grace emphasizes being saved (past tense) and ignores being saved (present tense). Christ's work on the cross is only one half of the salvation story. His resurrection and the sending of God's Spirit into our hearts is the second part of the good news. *The cross is God's mercy; His resurrection and Spirit within us is God's grace.*

The Bible emphasizes the distinction between living under the law and living in grace. Repeatedly, law and grace are contrasted as opposite ways of living.

> **You are not under law but under grace.** Romans 6:14

> *For the law was given through Moses;* **grace and truth came through Jesus Christ.** John 1:17

> *You are severed from Christ* [God's Spirit within you], *you who would be justified by the law;* **you have fallen away from grace** [God's divine influence upon your heart and His expression in and through your life]. *For through the Spirit* [within us], *by faith* [in Christ—God's Spirit in us], *we wait for the hope of righteousness* [Christ in and through us as our righteousness].
> Galatians 5:4-5

Instead of living in grace, we make Scriptures and beliefs our laws. We obey these laws rather than allowing God's Spirit to live in and through us.

In this book, I advocate what I believe to be a more accurate meaning of grace—one that provides greater depth of meaning and reveals how important living in grace is and what the early Christians were experiencing when they talked about grace.

A More Accurate Interpretation of Grace

The Greek word for "grace," *charis*, occurs 150 times in the New Testament, appearing more often than "saved" or "salvation." Grace even outnumbers the word for *agape* love.

In Strong's Concordance, grace is defined as follows:

> 5485. *charis*; graciousness of manner or act (abstract or concrete; literal, figurative or spiritual; especially the **divine influence upon the heart, and its reflection in the life**): acceptable, benefit, favor, gift, grace, gracious, joy, liberality, pleasure, thanks, thankworthy.

The words that leaped out to me as I read this definition of grace were the "divine influence upon the heart, and its reflection in the life." I believe this definition of grace is more complete than unmerited favor. It captures the essence of our faith and helps me understand why we cannot be under the law if we are living in grace.

In subsequent chapters, I show how this definition enriches the meaning of grace and brings to life verses in the Bible about our faith.

Let's just look at one important Scripture and see how this definition of grace sums up our faith. Ephesians 3:14-21 spells out the work of God, Christ, and the Holy Spirit in our life:

God's divine influence...

*For this reason I bow my knees before the Father, from whom every family in heaven and on earth is named, that according to the riches of His glory He may grant you to be **strengthened with might through His Spirit in the inner man**,*

Upon our heart...

*and that **Christ may dwell in your hearts through faith;** that you, being rooted and grounded in love, may have power to comprehend with all the saints what is the breadth and length and height and depth, and to know the love of Christ which surpasses knowledge,*

And His reflection in our life...

*that you may be filled with all the fulness of God. Now to Him who **by the power at work within us is able to do far more abundantly than all that we ask or think**, to Him be glory in the church and in Christ Jesus to all generations, for ever and ever.*

Webster's dictionary includes both definitions of grace:

1a. beneficence or generosity shown by God to man, especially *Divine favor unmerited* by man: the mercy of God as distinguished from His justice.

1b. a free gift of God to man for His regeneration or sanctification: *an influence emanating from God* and acting for the spiritual well-being of the recipient.

1c. a state of acceptance with or of being pleasing to God: enjoyment of *divine favor*.

1d. *a virtue or moral excellence regarded as coming from God*: a Christian virtue: *God as the source of grace*.

I hope to show that grace is God's Spirit influencing us from within to do His will. It is His work in and through us; not just a characteristic of God or a blessing He gives.

Living In Grace Is Not Optional

Grace is not just a part of our Christian faith; it is foundational. Paul clearly links grace with faith and salvation.

*For **by grace you have been saved through faith**; and this is not your own doing, it is the gift of God—not because of works, lest any man should boast.*
Ephesians 2:8-9

Paul warns believers about losing their salvation by returning to law and falling from grace.

*You are severed from Christ you who would be justified by the law, you have **fallen from grace**.* Galatians 5:4

This is a wake up call to pay attention to living in grace. In this verse it is clear that falling from grace is being severed from Christ. This verse, I believe, reveals that grace is better understood by the definition "divine influence upon the heart and its reflection in the life" than the accepted interpretation unmerited favor. Paul is writing to the Galatians who were trying to be justified by the law. They wanted to do works to be saved.

Like many Christians today, the Galatians wanted to *do* good and avoid evil. They did not realize that this very desire took them to the Tree of the Knowledge of Good and Evil and away from the Tree of Life—Christ's life within. Just as Adam and Eve wanted to know good and evil, so we today fall into this trap trying to be good and avoid evil. We take control and sever ourselves from the WORD within us to heed the law of good and bad without. Like these Galatians, we forget that Christ is our righteousness and it is only when He is reigning within—that is, we are obeying His voice from within—that we are righteous. It is not our own doing good, but our obedience to God's Spirit within us.

Often when Christians read the word "Christ" they associate the name with Jesus because after He was anointed with God's Spirit at His baptism, He became Jesus Christ—the anointed one. However, when Jesus was born, Mary and Joseph were told to call his name "Jesus" and that is His name.

In *Strong's Concordance* "Christ" is defined as follows:

> 5547. *Christos*: anointed, i.e. the Messiah, an epithet of Jesus Christ.

An epithet is a word or phrase expressing some quality or attribute, such as Richard the Lion-Hearted or Honest Abe where the epithets are Lion-Hearted and Honest. Jesus Christ means Jesus was *anointed* with God's Spirit.

Christians are the anointed ones—anointed with Christ—God's Spirit within. Jesus won our restoration to God the Father and as a result we have God's Spirit within us. When we live and walk as Jesus did in God's Spirit, then we are living in grace.

When we remember that Christ means anointed with God's Spirit, Scriptures that refer to Christ take on enlightened meaning as to how we are to live.

> *I have been crucified with Christ; it is no longer I who live, but Christ who lives in me.*   Galatians 2:20

Paul asked the Galatians a question we need to ask ourselves:

> *Did you receive the Spirit by **works of the law or by hearing with faith**? Are you so foolish? Having begun with the Spirit, are you now ending with the flesh.... Does He who supplies the Spirit to you and works miracles among you do so by **works of the law or by hearing with faith**?*   Galatians 3:2-5

Paul said that we received the Spirit of God by hearing with faith, that is, by believing that the Spirit of God is speaking from within and having faith to obey. Why are we still trying to obey the law? Christ is a *Living* Savior who lives within us and it is His righteousness that saves us when we obey. It is not our obeying Bible verses, which then become our law. The Bible was written to bring us to Christ—a *Living* Savior within—not to override Him.

We are to live by the Spirit within who teaches us all things. We are not to live in the flesh trying to be good. Jesus was righteous because He listened to the Spirit of God within Him and obeyed. His goodness and righteousness came from obeying God the Father. Like Jesus, our righteousness comes only from listening to the Spirit of God within us and obeying.

We live by grace—God's divine influence on our heart and His reflection in our life. Our work is to listen and obey—to have faith in the *Living* Savior within.

There is a great distinction between having Christian beliefs and believing in Christ—a *Living* being. For many Christians their beliefs have become laws.

There is a great difference between believing in written words in the Bible and believing the *Living Word*—Christ. The Bible was meant to bring us to Christ, not to replace Him with written words and beliefs. Believing is not about beliefs and creeds. Too often beliefs just become the new laws that prevent us from believing in Christ and entering into grace.

Beliefs are what make up every religion—all have words they believe and try to live by. Even philosophy is a belief in words. Only Christianity has a *Living* Savior and a *Living* God who come to live within.

Jesus made it possible for us to live in grace; He also showed us how to live in grace.

> *But to all who received Him, who believed in His name, He gave **power to become children of God; who were born**, not of blood nor of the will of the flesh nor of the will of man, but **of God**. And the Word became flesh and dwelt among us, **full of grace** and truth; we have beheld His glory, glory as of the only Son from the Father.... And **from His fulness have we all received, grace upon grace**. For the law was given through Moses; **grace and truth came through Jesus Christ**.*   *John 1:12-17*

Living in grace is not optional, not just a nice bonus in our faith. It is the essence of our faith. And if we do not enter into grace and remain under the law, we are not in God's kingdom and not appropriating what Christ did on the cross. We are denying Christ.

A Grace That Saves — My Experience

Let me tell you about my own experience with coming to understand grace.

In the past, whenever I was discouraged or going through a hard time, I would look in my Bible for words of encouragement. Often a Scripture would be quickened and I would grab onto it as my thought for the day. Although I am still tempted to open the Bible and look for verses for comfort and encouragement, I am learning a better way.

On one particular occasion when I was in a hurtful situation and feeling very weak, I came across the verse:

> *My grace is sufficient for you, for my power is made perfect in weakness.*   *2 Corinthians 12:9*

I consulted the Amplified Version of the Bible to get some understanding of what I should expect from sufficient grace:

My grace [my favor and loving-kindness and mercy] *is enough for you* [sufficient against any danger and enables you to bear the trouble manfully]; *for* My *strength* and *power are made perfect* [fulfilled and completed] *and show themselves most effective in* [your] *weakness.*   *2 Corinthians 12:9*

This amplification did not enlighten me. I still didn't know how to experience His strength or power. It just made me question further how is God's character of loving kindness and mercy helping me in this? If He is kind and loving, why am I suffering so with this? Why did He allow this?

I needed help and comfort. As I pondered this verse, I imagined God saving me from my circumstance. I looked for relief. When my relief didn't come, I was even more discouraged.

I recall that I was expecting my patronizing parent to come along side and fix my problem for me. I wanted some of this unmerited favor and blessing.

I now realize that this is not the way God works in our lives during difficult times. Sometimes He is the author of our difficulties. He engineers situations that cause troubles in our life to help us realize that our strength is in Him.

Having a better understanding of grace helped me ask better questions in these situations. Rather than asking for relief, I ask for His grace—a manifestation of His presence in my life.

Since I was not able to alter my situation and sought comfort, I was in a teachable moment. I wanted to know just how God's grace was sufficient for me. In this situation, God had an opportunity to reveal truth to me. Scriptures I thought I understood took on new meaning.

At this time I came to understand the deeper meaning of grace. How much richer and more honoring to Jesus' work of atonement is my understanding of this Scripture:

> *My grace* [presence in you] *is enough for you for my strength and power* [my influence and reigning in and through you] *are made perfect in your weakness* [when you give up control and surrender to me].
> 2 Corinthians 12:9

He is the answer. Relief from my situation is not the solution to my problem. I must live in grace and come to know my Living LORD within. I must come to rely on Him exclusively.

From this point on my quiet times became more an intimate conversation with my Living LORD than reading Scripture.

Reading Scripture to encourage oneself is not bad, but it must not replace going to God Himself and getting His strength in a situation. Reading about someone else's experiences in the Bible can be helpful but how much better to have God's perspective on your own situation. Claiming God's actions with a historical person in the Bible can be claiming Scripture and putting God to the test. We do not want to be bossing God around.

Many times I have had a situation where there was no clear direction in the Bible. Our God is the one who reveals His will for our life and He is alive within and seeking to do so.

Grace Is God's Spirit Working In and Through Us

Grace captures the essence of our salvation, our reconciliation with God our Father. Jesus paid the price so that we could again have God's Spirit united with us and live as Jesus did.

Grace is God's divine influence on our heart and His expression in and through us. This is the Good News. We are not left alone to try and live the law. We are set free by Christ and given love which fulfills all law by God our Father who is love. He did it all and He does it all. We need but cooperate by inviting Him into our lives and then submitting to His words and promptings. We need to acknowledge His presence and learn to hear and follow.

To live in grace we need to live from within—from God's Spirit within—rather than looking to authorities and laws without. Our walk becomes one of allowing God's Spirit expression in and through us.

Grace limited to unmerited favor causes Christians to expect God to bless them from without and to not appropriate the glorious gift they already have been given within. It causes us to abdicate our responsibilities to a remote God rather than experience His strength from within. Faith becomes hope in a concept of God instead of a relationship with our Father.

This belief also causes us to look to God to save us from difficult situations without listening or heeding His promptings. Prayer is our way of dropping the problem in God's lap and waiting for Him to fix the situation, but God is giving us guidance to take action. Our beliefs about faith and grace create a false hope of salvation without our involvement. In this way we do not learn to know the power that is within us and don't grow in faith. God is saying to us what He said to Moses, "You part the waters." If we don't know who resides within us and do not heed His promptings, we will stand at the edge of the Red Sea calling out to God to part the waters while He is looking for us to obey His command.

Grace Is a Gift That Must Be Received and Lived

Grace is a free gift, but a gift must be received. Just as salvation is a gift available to all, but only those who receive it are saved. So it is with grace.

Let's say that you are given a guide to lead you through a dangerous part of a foreign country. The guide is only useful if you believe in the guide and follow his instruction. So it is with salvation and grace. We receive the Spirit of God in our hearts but we must follow God's instructions and leadings to be saved. We must believe God's Spirit is in our heart and heed His voice from within. We must follow the motivations He puts in our heart.

Let's say my parents give me a bike as a birthday gift. The bike is a gift but if I don't receive the bike then the transaction is incomplete. A gift must pass from the giver to the recipient. If for some reason I don't believe they gave me the bike, then it is not really mine. And if I don't believe they gave it to me, it will probably sit in the garage unused. Or, if I don't believe I can ride it, again I have not received the gift. I must not only accept the bike but also use it. Likewise we must receive the gift of grace and believe by living in grace.

It is one thing to acknowledge mentally that we are under grace and not the law; it is another thing to live in grace. To live in grace we must believe that the Living God reigns in our hearts and will express Himself in our lives. To live in grace is to receive the gift: God working in and through us.

Living in grace means we believe God's love is poured into our hearts through the Holy Spirit.

> *Therefore, since we are justified by faith, we have peace with God through our Lord Jesus Christ.* **Through Him we have obtained access to this grace** *in which we stand, and we rejoice in our hope of sharing the glory of God. More than that, we rejoice in our sufferings, knowing that suffering produces endurance, and endurance produces character, and character produces hope, and hope does not disappoint us, because* **God's love has been poured into our hearts through the Holy Spirit which has been given to us.** *Romans 5:1-5*

We must choose to believe that we are reconciled to God our Father.

> *For if while we were enemies we were reconciled to God by the death of His Son, much more, now that* ***we are***

*reconciled, shall we be saved by His life. Not only so, but we also rejoice in God through our Lord Jesus Christ, through **whom we have now received our reconciliation**.* Romans 5:10-11

Grace is not ours until we receive and act on it. The writer of Hebrews warned them to make sure they obtained the grace of God.

See to it that no one fail to obtain the grace of God.
Hebrews 12:15

He knew that grace is available to us, but we have to appropriate it or we fall into sin. Receiving and entering into grace is allowing God in us to influence our heart and express Himself through us. In order to do this we must believe that God's Spirit is in us and will act.

To not receive grace is an act of pride. It is pride because we don't believe that God sent His Spirit into our hearts and wants to operate from there. Or, we believe His Spirit is in our heart but we refuse to submit, trusting our own decisions and actions more than His.

Receiving grace requires humility.

*Unfaithful creatures! Do you not know that friendship with the world is enmity with God? Therefore whoever wishes to be a friend of the world makes Himself an enemy of God. Or do you suppose it is in vain that the scripture says, "He yearns jealously over the **Spirit which He has made to dwell in us**"? But He gives more **grace**; therefore it says, "God opposes the proud, but gives **grace to the humble**." Submit yourselves therefore to God.* James 4:4-7

Humility is surrendering to God's divine influence within.

Grace and Faith Versus Law and Works

As Christians, we have been taught that we are saved by faith and not works. We also know that we are no longer under the law but under grace.

Knowing intellectually about grace and faith does not mean we have entered into the freedom Christ won for us.

We all know these Scriptures:

*For we hold that a man is justified by **faith apart from works of law**.*   Romans 3:28

*God, who is rich in mercy, out of the great love with which He loved us, even when we were dead through our trespasses, made us alive together with Christ (**by grace you have been saved**).... For **by grace you have been saved through faith**; and this is not your own doing, it is the gift of God—**not because of works**, lest any man should boast.*   Ephesians 2:4-9

*You are not under law but under **grace**.*   Romans 6:14

***We are discharged from the law**, dead to that which held us captive, so that we serve not under the old written code but **in the new life of the Spirit**.*
     Romans 7:6

***A man is not justified by works of the law but through faith in Jesus Christ**, even we have believed in Christ Jesus, in order to be justified by faith in Christ, and not by works of the law, because by works of the law shall no one be justified.*   Galatians 2:16

Yet, how many of us really live this way? How many of us still try to keep the law by trying to fulfill the do's and do not's we read in the Bible. How many of us still judge ourselves either good or bad based on the works we do? How many of us still cling to our beliefs, which often are just another word for laws? Have we really entered the grace Christ won for us?

You still might believe that grace is a characteristic of God—His gracious giving of blessings we don't deserve. But Scripture clearly states that grace comes through Jesus Christ—His work on the cross made it possible for us to receive this grace of God.

> *The law was given through Moses; **grace** and truth came through Jesus Christ.*   *John 1:17*

> *I give thanks to God always for you because of the **grace** of God which was given you in Christ Jesus.*
> *1 Corinthians 1:4*

The prophets of the Old Testament realized grace depended on Christ and saw that salvation was to be ours through grace.

> *The prophets who prophesied of the **grace** that was to be yours searched and inquired about this salvation.*
> *1 Peter 1:10*

What does it mean to live in grace and how does this relate to our faith? This is the theme of this book.

In subsequent chapters, we will examine the following questions and see how grace is foundational to our faith.

> What does it mean to have faith?
> What does it mean to live in grace?
> What does it mean to believe in Jesus?
> How do we follow Jesus?
> How do we obey God's voice?
> How do we do God's will?
> How do we love God with our all?

In answering these key questions, I have found that many Scriptures that I once found contradictory or confusing come alive and make perfect sense. For example, how can Scripture say we are saved by faith and not by works, yet faith without works is dead? How can Scripture say we are not saved by works yet say we will be judged by our works?

> *For we hold that a man is justified by faith apart from works of law.*   *Romans 3:28*

> *You see that a man is justified by works and not by faith alone.*   *James 2:24*

> *And all the churches shall know that I am He who searches mind and heart, and I will give to each of you as your works deserve.*   *Revelations 2:23*

> *For he will render to every man according to his works.*
>   *Romans 2:6*

As we look at grace from this new vantage point, the relationship between faith and works becomes clearer.

How can God say we are sinful and need forgiveness and yet say that when we are born of God and become His children we cannot sin? How can we believe we are sinless? Isn't it a sin even to think we are without sin—the ultimate in pride?

> *If we say we have no sin, we deceive ourselves, and the truth is not in us. If we confess our sins, He is faithful and just, and will forgive our sins and cleanse us from all unrighteousness. If we say we have not sinned, we make Him a liar, and His word is not in us.*
>   *1 John 1:8-10*

> *He who commits sin is of the devil; for the devil has sinned from the beginning. The reason the Son of God appeared was to destroy the works of the devil.* **No one born of God commits sin;** *for God's nature abides in*

*him, and **he cannot sin because he is born of God**.*
1 John 3:8-9

*No one who abides in **Him** sins; no one who sins has either seen Him or known Him.*   *1 John 3:6*

As we examine grace and relate it to our faith, we see that we are not only saved from our past sins, but we are also given power to not sin. If we don't believe we can be sinless, how do we reconcile these Scriptures from 1 John above?

What about the command to walk as Jesus did? How can we walk like He did when we see Jesus rebuking the Pharisees—calling them hypocrites and sons of their father the devil? This is not the way I think I am to speak and conduct myself according Scriptures that say I am to respect those over me and to love my neighbor. The Pharisees were the zealous religious leaders who taught the Scriptures and worked tirelessly to convert others to their beliefs. I have wondered why Jesus was so hard on the Pharisees and so kind to beggars and prostitutes. I wonder how He would respond to the zealous Christian leaders and Bible teachers of today. We will look at what makes us modern-day Pharisees and examine if we are one. Are we following beliefs or living in grace?

Other seemingly contradictory passages in the Bible deal with the unforgivable sin. The Bible says Christ died for all and has made a way for all to come to repentance. He provided a way for all sins to be forgiven. So why is blasphemy against Jesus forgivable but not blasphemy against the Holy Spirit?

*Therefore I tell you, every sin and blasphemy will be forgiven men, but **the blasphemy against the Spirit will not be forgiven**. And whoever says a word against the Son of man will be forgiven; but **whoever speaks against the Holy Spirit will not be forgiven**, either in this age or in the age to come.*   *Matthew 12:31-32*

I am learning that these contradictions occur because I lack understanding. When I applied my new understanding of grace to these seemingly contradictory Scriptures, they were wonderfully clarified. It was like an avalanche of understanding that made Scriptures come alive and truly be Good News.

As we go through the various aspects of grace, I will point out how each of these seemingly contradictory Scriptures make perfect sense when living in grace.

Living In Grace Is Faith

In this chapter, I have expressed my concerns about interpreting grace as unmerited favor and have given what I consider a more complete meaning. I have stressed why understanding grace is so critical to our faith.

In subsequent chapters, I go into more depth explaining how grace is the very essence of our faith and how this more accurate definition of grace relates to our salvation.

In Chapter 2, I discuss the significance of divine influence and how our faith and salvation are based on this prerequisite. We will look at what it means to have the kingdom of God within us and what it means for us to be the temple of the Living God. We will look at what it means to be *of God* and whether we are being truthful when we call Him LORD.

In Chapter 3, I show why God emphasizes the heart and not the mind. We will see why our heart is more critical to our faith and salvation than our mind. We examine what relationship God desires with us and why our heart must be the focus of His influence on our life.

In Chapter 4, I discuss how God expresses Himself in and through us when we make Him LORD. We will see that we are to live as Jesus did, doing only what God the Father said and did through Him. We will see how our salvation is not only from past sins but also from future sinning.

Chapter 5 closes our discussion about grace showing how Jesus manifested grace and how not living in grace has eternal consequences.

Sometimes I use the phrase "God wants to have control of our life" and this may disturb some of you. When I refer to God wanting to be *in control*, I really mean *influence* because God always gives us the power of choice. God only has the influence or control over our lives that we choose to give Him. God does not control us like a robot. He leads and speaks to us, but never forces us to do what He desires. He gives us the opportunity to live together with Him as LORD.

I use the word *control* because I want to emphasize that either God is in control or Satan is in control of our life. This is clearly stated throughout Scriptures. Our spirit is either of the Spirit of God or of the spirit of Satan. This is the spiritual battle that wages within us.

We deceive ourselves when we think we are in control of our lives. Self-in-control is really choosing to not let God be LORD and by default choosing to have Satan in control of our life. We choose to be of the flesh and of the world rather than of God.

I emphasize this repeatedly because God's Spirit reigning in our life is the essence of grace and our faith. God's divine influence upon our heart and His expression in and through our life is living in grace. This is faith.

I invite you to consider if you have fully entered into the gift of grace that Christ provides for you. In the following chapters, I will show how grace is the cornerstone of our faith by relating all the key elements of our faith to this richer understanding of grace. For me, understanding grace has brought a freedom and great joy in my spiritual walk that I never could have imagined. I realize now that I had been ignorant of what Jesus really had won for me and that I had been denying Christ in my life, yes, denying Christ. We deny Christ when we ignorantly or pridefully fail to enter into the salvation He won for us. We ignore or refuse the gift of grace.

Chapter 2: Divine Influence— God Reigning In Us

Living in grace begins by allowing God to have His rightful place in our lives.

Reconciliation With God Our Father

Christ's work on the cross gives each of us the opportunity to have God's presence within. Christ died to reconcile us to God our Father.

We can mentally acknowledge the Holy Spirit yet not enter into the reality of God being present in us. God is Spirit and the Holy Spirit available to us is God Himself.

We are to worship Him, which means giving Him our life and allowing Him to live in and through us, that is, allowing His divine influence upon our heart.

To receive the gift of grace we have to believe that Christ reunited us to our Father and believe that God's presence is within us and then live our lives accordingly. To ignore God's presence in us or to give only mental assent to this fact, is to deny Christ's work on the cross and His life in us.

Our great SIN is our separation from God. In the Garden of Eden, Adam and Eve chose to eat of the Tree of the Knowledge of Good and Evil so that they could make decisions on their own by knowing the difference between good and evil. They explicitly disobeyed God who told them not to eat of this tree. They separated themselves from God, who was within them, in order to make decisions about good and evil on their own. God designed them to follow Him, that is, His influence from within. He breathed His Spirit within Adam and Eve and gave them permission to eat of any tree in the garden, including the Tree of Life, which represents eternal life. They knew they were disobeying, but desired to be like God making decisions about what is good and what is evil. Adam and Eve chose to try to do good based on their knowledge of good and evil. They chose not to follow God's Spirit within, that is, follow God who is the only source of good.

Even Jesus didn't allow others to call Him good, but pointed to God, our Father, as the only one who is Good.

> *As he was setting out on his journey, a man ran up and knelt before him, and asked him, "Good Teacher, what must I do to inherit eternal life?" And Jesus said to him, "Why do you call me good? No one is good but God alone."* Mark 10:17-18

> *And a ruler asked him, "Good Teacher, what shall I do to inherit eternal life?" And Jesus said to him, "Why do you call me good? No one is good but God alone."*
> Luke 18:18-19

We too try to be good by knowing good and evil. We think we can become good by avoiding evil. *Good does not come from the avoidance of evil.* We are good only when God, who is good, is within us. It is only His goodness that makes us good. Just as Christ did not claim to be good and gave credit to God alone in Him, we too must realize that our goodness comes only from God, who is good. We have His goodness only if we receive God's Spirit and allow God to reign in our life. We have to give up our independent life of trying to do good and avoid doing evil to follow God's guidance and influence from within. God alone is good.

*From now on, therefore, we regard no one from a human point of view; even though we once regarded Christ from a human point of view, we regard him thus no longer. Therefore, **if any one is in Christ, he is a new creation**; the old has passed away, behold, the new has come. All this is from God, who through Christ reconciled us to himself and gave us the ministry of reconciliation; that is, in Christ God was reconciling the world to himself, not counting their trespasses against them, and entrusting to us the message of reconciliation. So we are ambassadors for Christ, God making his appeal through us. We beseech you on behalf of Christ, be reconciled to God. For our sake he made him to be sin who knew no sin, so that in him we might become the righteousness of God. Working together with him, then, **we entreat you not to accept the grace of God in vain**. For he says, "At the acceptable time I have listened to you, and helped you on the day of salvation." Behold, now is the acceptable time; behold, now is the day of salvation.*   2 Corinthians 5:16-6:2

Christ reconciled us to our Father God, but we need to enter into grace in order for Christ's sacrifice to not go in vain.

Grace Is a Matter of Life or Death

We don't always realize our precarious condition. We tend to think of ourselves as good people and so we are content to live our religion by being good and avoiding evil. We even judge ourselves by what we consider good and evil, which is eating off the Tree of the Knowledge of Good and Evil, In other words, we are under the law.

Laws define good and evil. Without laws there is no defining good and evil. Try thinking of something you do that is good and explain what you base your decision on. Do the same for something you think is evil. It always comes back to laws.

We don't realize we are under the law when we obey verses in the Bible. We are blind to the fact that obeying written Scriptures is just another set of laws which are beliefs. Yes, our beliefs become our laws and we judge ourselves based on these beliefs. This is the way of the world, not God's definition of good and evil. Let me explain.

God created man in the Garden of Eden and breathed life into him.

> *So God created man in his own image, in the image of God he created him; male and female he created them.*
> *Genesis 1:27*
>
> *Then the LORD God formed man of dust from the ground, and breathed into his nostrils the breath of life; and man became a living being.* *Genesis 2:7*

God gave them life by putting His Spirit within them. God's Spirit is life. To not have God's Spirit within us is to be dead.

In the garden, Adam and Eve took of the Tree of the Knowledge of Good and Evil. We think of this as the first sin that brought judgment on us all. This was not just a sin as we think of sins. Recall what God asks of them and what He said would be the consequence:

> *The LORD God commanded the man, saying, "You may freely eat of every tree of the garden; but of the tree of the knowledge of good and evil you shall not eat, for in the day that you eat of it **you shall die**." Genesis 2:16-17*

He didn't say they would have some discipline for disobeying. He stated it clearly: they would die.

We know Adam and Eve understood what God commanded them because Eve repeats God's command.

> *Now the serpent was more subtle than any other wild creature that the LORD God had made. He said to the woman, "Did God say, 'You shall not eat of any tree of the garden'?" And the woman said to the serpent, "We may eat of the fruit of the trees of the garden; but God said, 'You shall not eat of the fruit of the tree which is in the midst of the garden, neither shall you touch it, lest you die.'" But the serpent said to the woman, "**You will not die**. For God knows that when you eat of it your eyes will be opened, and you will be like God, **knowing good and evil**."* Genesis 3:1-5

Satan incited Eve to question God and deceived her to believe a lie. He said she would not die but be like God knowing good and evil. She would know good and evil but she, by her disobedience of God's command, would be separated from God, the only source of good and fall under the control of Satan who is the source of evil.

Adam and Eve died that day and we as their descendents died with them. Once man had control, or thought he had control, man became a slave of sin and the laws of good and evil—right and wrong.

We too have this same tendency. As professing Christians we want to do good and not evil. The problem is we are blind to how to do good and avoid evil. We mistakenly think that we can do it on our own. We think that God is asking us to do it on our own. We might profess that we trust in God's Spirit but we don't really know how to let the Spirit of God in us be in charge. We give mental assent but we still cling to our performance system of trying to be good and not bad. We still take of the Tree of the Knowledge of Good and Evil, the Tree of Death, and fail to realize that we need to take of the Tree of Life.

Adam and Eve were not prohibited from eating of the Tree of Life. They could have chosen life but they chose death. As a result, they became walking corpses—dead but still believing they were alive. Life and death is about who reigns in our life—sin and death or grace and life. Sin and death reign when we are separated from God. Either God reigns and we live in grace or death reigns.

> *Therefore as sin came into the world through one man and **death through sin**, and so death spread to all men because all men sinned—sin indeed was in the world before the law was given, but sin is not counted where there is no law. Yet death reigned from Adam to Moses, even over those whose sins were not like the transgression of Adam, who was a type of the one who was to come. But the free gift is not like the trespass. For if many died through one man's trespass, much more have the **grace of God** and **the free gift in the grace** of that one man Jesus Christ abounded for many. And the free gift is not like the effect of that one man's sin. For the judgment following one trespass brought condemnation, but the free gift following many trespasses brings justification. If, because of one man's trespass, death reigned through that one man, much more will those **who receive the abundance of grace and the free gift of righteousness** reign in life through the one man Jesus Christ. Then as one man's trespass led to condemnation for all men, so one man's act of righteousness leads to acquittal and life for all men. For as by one man's disobedience many were made sinners, so by one man's obedience many will be made righteous. Law came in, to increase the trespass; but where sin increased, **grace abounded all the more**, so that, as sin reigned in death, **grace also might reign through righteousness** to eternal life through Jesus Christ our Lord.*   *Romans 5: 12-21*

Many so-called Christians are still dead because they have not received God's gift of grace. Today these Christians have their beliefs, but have yet to *believe* in God our Father who is a *living* LORD who desires to reign in their hearts. They read Scriptures but do not trust themselves to listen to their *living* LORD. As a result they remain at the Tree of death and refuse to trust the Tree of Life.

Adam and Eve did not obey God's command. This was not a written law; it was the command of God spoken to them. Law did not come until Moses. Disobedience to the voice of God was the issue, as it is today. God is not asking us to keep the law, nor the beliefs we get about good and bad from the Bible. He is asking us to obey His voice—His commands—His words. Our God is *alive* and speaking. We are the ones who don't think we need to listen because we have our Bible. We ignore the *living* God and replace Him with written words. We too fall into the trap of Phariseeism by living the written words and refusing to come to the *living* WORD.

The only command in the garden of Eden was "Don't eat of the Tree of the Knowledge of Good and Evil." With this one disobedience, man was separated from God.

The laws given to Moses were to show man his need for God and to keep man from destroying himself until he repented and returned to God.

The law is meant to show us our condition so that we realize we are dead and return to God. Law is meant to show us that we are not capable of being good by knowing good and evil and trying to be good.

Law shows us our SIN of separation from God. SIN exists without law.

> *Sin indeed was in the world before the law was given, but sin is not counted where there is no law. Yet death reigned from Adam to Moses.*   *Romans 5:13-14*
>
> *For no human being will be justified in his sight by works of the law, since through the law comes knowledge of sin.*   *Romans 3:20*

Our sin comes not from violation of laws of good and evil but from our separation from God. Why then do we try to obey the law?

Trying to keep God's law will never keep us from sinning; in fact, the law actually causes us to sin.

> *What then shall we say? That the law is sin? By no means! Yet, if it had not been for the law, I should not have known sin. I should not have known what it is to covet if the law had not said, "You shall not covet." But sin, finding opportunity in the commandment, wrought in me all kinds of covetousness. Apart from the law sin lies dead. I was once alive apart from the law, but when the commandment came, sin revived and I died; the very commandment which promised life proved to be death to me. For sin, finding opportunity in the commandment, deceived me and by it killed me. So the law is holy, and the commandment is holy and just and good. Did that which is good, then, bring death to me? By no means! It was sin, working death in me through what is good, in order that sin might be shown to be sin, and through the commandment might become sinful beyond measure.*
>   *Romans 7:7-13*

Yes, laws can cause us to sin even though the law is God-given and holy. Why? Our response to the law causes us to sin. Instead of looking to God our Father for power to not sin, we try by will power to avoid evil and do good. We do just the opposite of depending on God; we depend even more on ourselves. Why? Because we think we are capable of keeping the law because we know good and evil. Our taste from the Tree of the Knowledge of Good and Evil blinds us to our true condition. We are dead because we are separated from God, the source of life. Dead means we are spiritually dead; God's Spirit is not in us.

We are like rebellious children who want to do it on their own, refusing the assistance of their parent. We are enamored with self-control and our ability to do good and avoid evil. As Christians, we take sin to be just an infraction that is easily rectified by confessing our sin. We often fail to see that we have yet to become Christian—that is live like Jesus did, dependent totally on the Spirit of God within Him. God the Father reigning in Jesus' life was the only source of His sinless nature. To be Christian we have to submit to God our Father as Jesus did.

God gave Adam and Eve a choice between the Tree of Life and the Tree of Death. We too have this choice of life and living in grace or death and living under the laws of good and evil.

We do not become like Christ by trying to be good and avoid evil. We become like Christ by listening and obeying the *living* God within who desires to influence our life for good.

Grace is the return of God's Spirit and His life within our being. Jesus made it possible for the Spirit of God to be available to us and for us to listen and obey God. Jesus fulfilled the law and provided the way to being reborn of God's Spirit. He freed us from the domain of Satan and death and restored us to the realm of God and eternal life. Jesus made it possible for us to be restored to God our Father—to be one with His Spirit.

To Live In Grace We Have to Lose Our Life

Now that we know we are dead, why does Scripture repeatedly say we must die to live. If we are already dead, why would we have to die to live?

When I read the following Bible verses, I wonder what it means to lose my life.

> *For whoever would save his life will lose it, and whoever loses his life for my sake will find it. For what will it profit a man, if he gains the whole world and forfeits his life? Or what shall a man give in return for his life?*
> Matthew 16:25-26

> *For whoever would save his life will lose it; and whoever loses his life for my sake and the gospel's will save it. For what does it profit a man, to gain the whole world and forfeit his life?* Mark 8:35-36

> *For whoever would save his life will lose it; and whoever loses his life for my sake, he will save it. For what does it profit a man if he gains the whole world and loses or forfeits himself?* Luke 9:24-25

Whenever I see something repeated in the Bible I like to make sure I understand what is meant. So what does it mean to lose our life in order to find it?

My understanding is that we are deceived into thinking we can have life without God's Spirit in charge. We acknowledge God's existence, but we do not let Him reign in our life. We remain in control.

We define life by our relationships with family and friends or by our work and accomplishments. Some of us define our life by recognition from the world in the form of income, prestige, or authority. Some of us seek security or independence as our interpretation of life.

Our bondages to this world's values is the life we must lose to enter into true life.

> *Truly, truly, I say to you, unless a grain of wheat falls into the earth and dies, it remains alone; but if it dies, it bears much fruit.* ***He who loves his life loses it, and he who hates his life in this world will keep it for eternal life.*** *John 12:24-25*

> *Those who live according to the flesh set their minds on the things of the flesh, but those who live according to the Spirit set their minds on the things of the Spirit.* ***To set the mind on the flesh is death, but to set the mind on the Spirit is life and peace.*** *For the mind that is set on the flesh is hostile to God; it does not submit to God's law, indeed it cannot; and those who are in the flesh cannot please God. But you are not in the flesh, you are in the Spirit, if in fact the Spirit of God dwells in you. Any one who does not have the Spirit of Christ does not belong to him.... So then, brethren, we are debtors, not to the flesh, to live according to the flesh—for if you live according to the flesh you will die, but if* ***by the Spirit you put to death the deeds of the body you will live.*** *Romans 8:5-13*

Only God's Spirit gives life. Worldly pleasures do not give life.

Once we get serious about our faith and give God His rightful place in our life, He begins the process of sanctification— purification, cleaning out, consecration, making us holy. With our permission, He begins the process of purging these values we used to call life and replaces them with His life.

This often comes as a surprise to Christians who believe that living in grace is to be blessed by God with worldly things.

When God starts to purge some of these gods from our life, we often murmur and resist His work. We hold tenaciously to family, status, money, possessions, etc., believing that these constitute the blessings of God. Instead we must realize that grace is God Himself and that fleshly values separate us from God. Yes, separate us from Him. How often have I violated my heart and the Spirit of God in me to carry out a belief I have about worldly success or being a good family member? When we violate the Spirit of God within to please man or carry out some obligation, we separate ourselves from God within. We live our beliefs—our laws—and fail to believe in our *living* LORD within.

Jesus said that He was not of this world and that those who follow Him are not of this world. Listen to His words concerning those who are of this world and those who are not of this world.

> *I have given them thy word; and* **the world has hated them because they are not of the world***, even as I am not of the world. I do not pray that thou shouldst take them out of the world, but that thou shouldst keep them from the evil one.* **They are not of the world, even as I am not of the world.** *John 17:14-16*

> *If you were of the world, the world would love its own; but because* **you are not of the world***, but I chose you out of the world,* **therefore the world hates you***.*
> *John 15:19*

We are either of this world or of God. We cannot have both. Many so-called Christians desire the things of this world and want to be loved by this world. Jesus plainly says we have a choice to make and each of us makes this choice.

Why don't people jump at the chance to have God, the creator of the universe, as the *divine influence* of their life? I believe it is because we love the things of this world and are unwilling to let go of them. We want God to bless us with things of this world. This is one reason unmerited favor appeals to so many Christians and why *divine influence upon our heart* is not so appealing. Our heart is occupied with enticements of this world that we believe are our life. We are content with our understanding of grace as unmerited favor, because it fits our lifestyle. We gloss over the following Scripture:

> *Do not love the world or the things in the world. If any one loves the world, love for the Father is not in him. For all that is in the world, the lust of the flesh and the lust of the eyes and the pride of life, **is not of the Father but is of the world**.*   1 John 2:15-16

> *Unfaithful creatures! Do you not know that **friendship with the world is enmity with God**? Therefore whoever wishes to be **a friend of the world makes himself an enemy of God**.*   James 4:4

Satan is in control of the world. Therefore our desires for the things of the world cause us to be followers of Satan and enemies of God.

> *And you he made alive, when you were dead through the trespasses and sins in which you once walked, following the course of this world, following the prince of the power of the air, the spirit that is now at work in the sons of disobedience. Among these we all once lived in the passions of our flesh, following the desires of body and mind, and so we were by nature children of wrath, like the rest of mankind. But God, who is rich in mercy, out of the great love with which he loved us, even when we were dead through our trespasses, **made us alive together with Christ (by grace you have been saved)**.*   Ephesians 2:1-5

Only God's presence within and His influence from within saves us. He is our only security. Only He is Life and life abundant. This is the life Jesus spoke of when He said:

> *I came that they may have **life**, and have it abundantly.*
>
> *John 10:10*

Either God Reigns or Satan Is In Control

The truth is we either surrender our life to God or Satan has control of our life. There is no other option. Being in control of our own life is the same as refusing to let God be Lord of our life and therefore to remain in our fallen state.

I didn't realize the importance of this until late in my walk with the LORD. I wanted to do what is good but I thought it was up to me to do good and thereby please God. Through will power I tried to do all that I knew to do. My definition of good came from obeying the laws and the authorities in my life.

I had been trained to believe that self-control was a godly virtue and that all my efforts were getting me somewhere in my Christian walk. I had no idea of how to let God be Lord of my life. I repeated the words, "Thy will be done," but hoped against hope that I was doing His will.

When I saw many verses about being of God or of Satan and the contrast of being of God or of the world and of the flesh, I began to wonder what it meant to be of God. I had blindly assumed it meant that if I had received Jesus as my Savior I was by definition of God.

I didn't realize that Christ's salvation and reconciliation with God required me to allow God to be Lord of my life. Like Jesus, I was to let God work in and through me. I was not to try to be good on my own because I cannot. I can only be good by allowing God to express His goodness through me. Me in control was really Satan in control of my life. I was still living as if I was separated from God.

Like most Christians, I believed I received the Holy Spirit as part of my salvation, but I had little understanding about the Holy Spirit's role in my daily life. I've included a few Scriptures here that made me realize the polarity between being of God or being of the flesh and of the world.

> *For those who live according to the flesh set their minds on the things of the flesh, but those who live according to the Spirit set their minds on the things of the Spirit. To set the mind on the flesh is death, but to set the mind on the Spirit is life and peace. For the mind that is set on the flesh is hostile to God; it does not submit to God's law, indeed it cannot; and those who are in the flesh cannot please God. But you are not in the flesh, you are in the Spirit, if in fact the Spirit of God dwells in you.*
> Romans 8:5-9

> *But I say, walk by the Spirit, and do not gratify the desires of the flesh. For the desires of the flesh are against the Spirit, and the desires of the spirit are against the flesh; for these are opposed to each other, to prevent you from doing what you would.*
> Galatians 5:16-17

> *Jesus answered, "Truly, truly, I say to you, unless one is born of water and the Spirit, he cannot enter the kingdom of God. That which is born of the flesh is flesh, and that which is born of the spirit is spirit."* John 3:5-6

> *For all that is in the world, the lust of the flesh and the lust of the eyes and the pride of life, is not of the Father but is of the world.* 1 John 2:16

I wondered why Jesus and the Pharisees were at such odds since the Pharisees were trying to obey the laws that God had laid down for them. I identified with these Pharisees in that I too was trying to be good by obeying laws I found in the Bible. Confronted with these words of Christ to the Pharisees, my wondering turned to an intense search to understand what it meant to be of God. I include Christ's words to these religious leaders here for you to ponder and ask yourself whether you are of God or still of Satan.

> *Jesus said to them, "If God were your Father, you would love me, for I proceeded and came forth from God; I came not of my own accord, but he sent me. Why do you not understand what I say? It is because you cannot bear to hear my word.* **You are of your father the devil**, *and your will is to do your father's desires. He was a murderer from the beginning, and has nothing to do with the truth, because there is no truth in him. When he lies, he speaks according to his own nature, for he is a liar and the father of lies. But, because I tell the truth, you do not believe me. Which of you convicts me of sin? If I tell the truth, why do you not believe me?* **He who is of God hears the words of God; the reason why you do not hear them is that you are not of God."** *John 8:42-47*

Are you still trying to be good or are you relying on God's presence in you? Have you submitted to God? Do you hear the words of God—the words of your *living* God from within?

In these beginning chapters, I show how all encompassing this word *grace* is to our faith. In subsequent chapters we will deal with the specifics of how to live moment by moment heeding the voice of God and His promptings.

Obedience from the Heart

God isn't asking us to obey a set of rules and then judging us on our ability to perform. This was not His intention when He created us and it is not His intention now.

God did not create Adam and Eve and give them rules to live by. He breathed His Spirit within them and thus they were good, in fact, Scripture says "very good." Adam and Eve *knew* God, who is good, and, as a result, were experiencing only good. They did not know evil.

God asked them not to eat of the Tree of the Knowledge of Good and Evil to keep them from knowing evil. God, who desired a love relationship, gave man the power of choice to be one with Him by heeding His leading from within or separating from Him. When man disobeyed God and chose Satan's leading to eat from the Tree of the Knowledge of Evil, man suffered the consequence of separation from God and spiritual death. Today, many of us are still enslaved under the laws of good and evil.

God did not write laws until about 2000 years after creation. When He did, the people of Israel wanted Moses to hear from God and then tell them what they were to do. They chose to listen to a human authority instead of God. Later, they wanted a king instead of God to lead and protect them. They wanted an intermediary between themselves and God.

How many Christians today want to rely on ordained pastors to be their spiritual guide and have little interest in hearing the voice of God for themselves? When we have no interest in hearing God's voice, we choose to separate ourselves from God by listening and following man and laws.

Jesus came to save us from ourselves—our independent selves. He not only showed us how to live by God's Spirit as the divine influence by which He lived, He also defeated Satan's hold on us. He made it possible for us to be reunited with God our

Father. He ushered in grace by fulfilling the law and forgiving our sins. He reconciled us to God our Father so that God's Spirit could live in us.

We either obey God's Spirit within or we obey Satan. *Law is self-control; grace is God in control.* Self-control is a deception because it is really Satan in control. We either choose to live under *God's divine influence* or we remain under the influence of Satan and are enslaved to sin. You might not like the word "slave" but we are slaves to Satan and sin or slaves of God and righteousness.

> *What then? Are we to sin because **we are not under law but under grace**? By no means! Do you not know that if you yield yourselves to any one as obedient slaves, **you are slaves of the one whom you obey**, either of sin, which leads to death, or of obedience, which leads to righteousness?... But thanks be to God, that **you who were once slaves of sin have become obedient from the heart**.... But now that **you have been set free from sin and have become slaves of God**, the return you get is sanctification and its end, eternal life. For the wages of sin is death, but the free gift of God is eternal life in Christ Jesus our Lord.*   Romans 6: 15-23

We are to obey God in a manner that a slave would yield to his master—not with eye-service but obedient from the heart.

> *Slaves, be obedient to those who are your earthly masters, with fear and trembling, in singleness of heart, as to Christ; not in the way of eye-service, as men-pleasers, but as servants of Christ, doing the will of God from the heart, rendering service with a good will as to the Lord and not to men.*   Ephesians 6:5-7

The key word in these Scriptures is obedient. I was surprised to find out that the Greek word for obedience does not mean keeping some law but hearkening to someone's voice. I have included Strong's Concordance definition of obedient here so you can see for yourself what it means to obey.

> 5218. *ypakoē hupakoe;* from 5219; **attentive hearkening**, i.e. (by implication) compliance or submission:—obedience, obedient, obeying.
>
> 5219. *ypakouō hupakouo;* from 5259 and 191; **to hear under (as a subordinate), i.e. to listen attentively; by implication, to heed or conform to a command or authority:—hearken**, be obedient to, obey.

I have highlighted the words *attentive hearkening* and *to hear and listen attentively*. This is what God is asking of us when He asks us to obey. He is asking us to listen attentively to His voice and to obey the commands He gives us. We are to be attentive to His presence in our heart. We are to be obedient from the heart.

> *Now we are discharged from the law, dead to that which held us captive, so that we serve not under the old written code but in the new life of the Spirit. Romans 7:6*

We no longer serve God through the written laws but in the new life of God's Spirit within.

Repentance Is Not a One Time Event

How do we make the shift from being under the law to being led by the Spirit of the *living* God? We repent and turn from our trying to live the law to God and His divine influence within.

When I heard the word *repent*, I thought of those non-Christians who need to repent. I did not think of my own need to repent. I had associated repentance with coming to Christ in the first place and that from then on it was a matter of forgiveness for my sins. Repentance, for me, was a one-time event.

I have since come to realize that repentance is what I need to repeatedly do because I readily wander from God's presence and take back control of my life.

Sometimes we take control in our zealousness to please God by doing good works for Him. We decide to do something good. We define *good* by our beliefs gleaned from the Bible. The problem is we decide what is good and do it on our own, not based on following God's Spirit within. We do our work and not God's work. We try to *do good* rather than *be good*, which is God expressed in and through our being.

Often fear is the reason we take back control from God. Fear is the opposite of faith. Looking at evil makes us fearful and then we try to overcome it. When we look at evil and try to avert or overcome it, we inadvertently take back control from God by trying to figure out what to do by ourselves.

God showed me that I cannot look at evil and Him at the same time. Evil is from Satan. God and Satan are infinitely far apart. I am either looking at God and good or I am looking at the devil and evil. Faith and fear are the motivators that make me look either to God or to the devil.

Let me illustrate this with a chart that has been helpful for me to carry around in my memory:

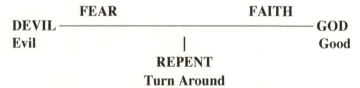

Repent literally means to turn around. Since we can't be looking at the devil and his work at the same time we are looking to God, we need to do an about face when we sense the warning signal of fear. When I am fearful, I have been listening to the enemy and need to repent and turn around to God and faith.

This may appear to be a minor issue, but I have seen how the enemy is very crafty in deceiving Christians to believe that this situation calls for forgiveness rather than repentance. In this way, the enemy keeps us in a vicious cycle of forgiveness of sins by keeping us separate from the only person who can make us sinless—God Himself. God alone is good and perfect and it is only His presence and His divine influence in our life that keeps us from sinning.

Yes, we have forgiveness of our sins through Christ's death and resurrection, but God never intended to leave us in this vicious cycle of sin-forgiveness-sin-forgiveness for the rest of our life. He had in mind something much better. He envisioned us living as Jesus did with total dependency on Himself, our Father. He breathed His Spirit in us at creation and He made His Spirit available again with Jesus' death and resurrection. Jesus paid for our sins, but this does not mean we continue in the cycle of sinning and asking forgiveness. No, we are given freedom *from* sinning through living in GRACE—God's divine influence on our heart and His expression in and through our life. This is the "NOT I BUT CHRIST IN ME" life that Paul writes about.

> *By the* **grace of God** *I am what I am, and* **his grace** *toward me was not in vain. On the contrary, I worked harder than any of them, though it was not I, but the* **grace of God which is with me**.   *I Corinthians 15:10*

Repentance returns us to GRACE. Forgiveness often leads to more self-control and the desire to not sin again. This self-control only leads to more sinning. If we have something we don't like about ourselves, we tend to crank up our willpower to overcome it. This causes us to fall away from the *living* God and return to self-effort and keeping laws.

First, we have to deal with the SIN of separation from God; then we can ask for forgiveness for continually doing it on our own. *Our sins are just a manifestation of our SIN—separation from*

God. Without repentance, we will remain in an endless cycle of sin-forgiveness-sin-forgiveness because forgiveness is not restoration of God's Spirit as our *divine influence*. More than likely, our forgiveness will just lead us to try to not do that sin again—a resolution we can never keep without God's presence in us and His divine influence on our heart.

SIN ⟶ sins
(Separation from God)

Our SIN is our primary problem; our sins are a secondary problem caused by our SIN. Repentance removes the SIN and therefore the sins. Keeping connected to the only source of good is the key. Our salvation and freedom come from the restoration of God's Spirit in our life. We have the choice to receive God's Spirit and submit to God or to remain independent by trying to be good.

Because this is so important, I want to emphasize what I just said about repentance and forgiveness because many Christians don't understand this.

Living the Christian life isn't about continually asking for forgiveness for the sins we commit, but about receiving a new creation with God as the command center of our life. With God reigning, we do not sin because He cannot sin. Our sinning is the result of our SIN: our separation from God.

People who consider themselves Christians believe that they repent once and forever after are of God and forever saved. What they fail to realize is that God is Lord only if we allow Him to do so. He gave us choice to listen and follow or to go it alone. I'm sorry to say that most of us prefer to go it alone and have God support our decisions. We, like Adam and Eve, prefer to control our own lives by avoiding evil and doing good. We fail to understand that only God is GOOD and all our attempts to be good are the good works of a Pharisee.

I am concerned that Satan focuses us on forgiveness of sins as the way to salvation to keep us from realizing our need for repentance. He does this by convincing us that we will always sin and therefore need forgiveness of sins, that is, a pardon from the punishment for our sins. We do need to be pardoned, but we have lost sight of the need for repentance, which is turning from Satan to God. When we are of God, we don't sin and therefore don't need pardoning of our sins. If we don't repent, we continue to sin and ask for forgiveness, a cycle that never ends.

In the past I believed I needed to have all of my sins forgiven, but I could not come up with a scenario where this could be true. Let me explain. We Christians have an underlying belief that we must ask for forgiveness for all the sins we commit in order to enter into the pardon that Christ won for us. If we fail to realize that it is Christ's living presence in us giving us cessation from sinning, then we are always in a state of unforgiven sins.

Ask yourself if you are sinless at the present moment. Do you question or doubt whether you can ever be sinless? If so, then you have this underlying belief in your need for pardon from the sins you commit and that you can never get into a sinless state. It is true you cannot be sinless by asking for forgiveness of sins repeatedly, but you can by making God the divine influence of your life. With God reigning within, He makes you sinless. This is the significance of Christ's work on the cross and our restoration with God the Father.

Satan's ploy is to keep us thinking that we do not need repentance because we are Christians and have already received Jesus Christ. Therefore, Satan can keep us separated from God and continually sinning. So, we keep asking for forgiveness to erase sins from God's books. We also try to save ourselves by attempting to keep ourselves from sinning by willpower, which is self-control and being in the grip of Satan. We may get a measure of control over one sin, but Satan has many sins he can tempt us with, and we will spend the rest of our lives trying not to sin and remaining in control of our lives.

God, on the other hand, is concerned about our separation from Him, which is the cause of all sins. Separation from God is the big SIN, which causes all other sins. Therefore, God would have us concentrate on surrendering to Him so that we don't sin. Someone born of God cannot sin. Therefore, if we can eliminate the SIN—separation from God—we need not concern ourselves with sins. If we see that we are sinning, we should recognize our need to repent and be reunited with God rather than trying to eliminate our sinning. To eliminate sins ourselves we take control and this is the cause of all sinning—self in control.

Repentance is the way of returning to God's grace—His divine influence upon our heart and His expression in and through us.

The Kingdom of God Is Within Us

Our job is to invite God into our life and then submit to His divine influence. This involves humbly submitting to His Spirit by believing that God is in us and obeying His promptings. Paul said it well when he appealed to the Romans to present their bodies a living sacrifice as worship of God.

> *I appeal to you therefore, brethren, by the mercies of God, to **present your bodies as a living sacrifice**, holy and acceptable **to God, which is your spiritual worship**. Do not be conformed to this world but be transformed by the renewal of your mind, that you may prove what is the will of God, what is good and acceptable and perfect.*
> *Romans 12:1-2*

A king reigns in his kingdom. Wherever God reigns is His kingdom. Therefore, if you allow God to reign in your life, His kingdom is within you.

Establishing God's kingdom in our life needs to be our first priority. Jesus expressed it this way:

> **Seek first God's kingdom** *and his righteousness, and all these things shall be yours as well.* Matthew 6:33

In the past when I read "kingdom of God" in the Bible, I would think of heaven some day. Now these very words well up in me an inexpressible gratefulness that the God of the universe would come and live within me and save me. The Almighty God gave me a new heart with His Spirit such that I am able to do His will. My Heavenly Farther loves me so much He wants to be one with me and allow me to participate in His life. That is Good News!

When you read "kingdom of God" in Scripture, remember this kingdom is within you if you allow God to be LORD of your life, that is, to reign in your heart. This is a treasure worth everything we now count valuable.

> *The* **kingdom of heaven** *is like a merchant in search of fine pearls, who, on finding one* **pearl of great value**, *went and* **sold all that he had and bought it.**
> Matthew 13:45-46

Entering this kingdom is not difficult; it requires our humble submission to God our Father by obeying His Spirit within our heart. We are to become like children who understand that our Father is in charge and that we are to obey Him.

> *Calling to him a child, he put him in the midst of them, and said, "Truly, I say to you,* **unless you turn and become like children, you will never enter the kingdom of heaven.** *Whoever humbles himself like this child, he is the greatest in the kingdom of heaven."* Matthew 18:2-4

The importance of our becoming like children is repeated in Mark and Luke.

> *Truly, I say to you,* **whoever does not receive the kingdom of God like a child shall not enter it.**
>
> Mark 10:15; Luke 18:17

Children look to their parents as their authority. Only rebellious children try to go it on their own. We too are not meant to leave our Father and go it alone. We were designed to have God's Spirit within us and to obey His voice and promptings.

LORD Means God Is Reigning Within

Often we use the word *LORD* as just another name for God or Christ, yet we do not make God or Christ LORD of our life.

God does not force us to obey Him. He gave us *choice* to listen and obey or live our life separate from Him. The choice is ours, but the consequences of not making Him LORD is a matter of being saved or not.

God commands us to have no other gods before Him. This includes not making His laws a god replacing Him in our life. This was a major sin of the religious leaders of Christ's day. The Pharisees prided themselves on keeping the law and saw no need for Christ and salvation. Our God is a *living* God, not a concept. He is *alive* and has created us to operate properly with His Spirit within us. We were never intended to operate separate from God or to submit to any other authority. LORD means LORD—the ultimate authority.

The word *Lord* appears 7800 times in the Bible; 650 times in the New Testament. I'd say *Lord* is an important word to understand.

Strong's Concordance gives the following definition for the Greek word "Lord":

> 2962. *kyrios kurios;* from *kyros kuros* (**supremacy**); **supreme in authority**, i.e. (as noun) **controller**; by

implication, Master (as a respectful title):—God, Lord, master, Sir.

In Webster's dictionary Lord is defined as follows;

Someone having **power, authority, or influence**
A **master** or **ruler**
A name for God or Christ

The Thesaurus lists the following words as synonyms for lord: master, ruler, leader, chief, superior, monarch, sovereign, king, emperor, prince, governor, commander.

Whatever interpretation you choose to use, it means the person in charge. Is God the sovereign of your life? Are you speaking the truth when you refer to Him as Lord?

Jesus rebuked the religious people of His day with:

*"Why do you call me 'Lord, Lord,' and not do what I tell you? Every one who comes to me and **hears my words** and does them, I will show you what he is like: he is like a man building a house, who dug deep, and laid the foundation upon rock; and when a flood arose, the stream broke against that house, and could not shake it, because it had been well built. But **he who hears** and does not do them is like a man who built a house on the ground without a foundation; against which the stream broke, and immediately it fell, and the ruin of that house was great."* Luke 6:46-49

Calling God Lord is saying you are listening and heeding His voice. In the Scripture above, Jesus describes this as the solid foundation upon which faith is built. "Hears my words" isn't referring to hearing God's word through someone else. It means hearing God speak to you. Can you hear God's voice? If not, what are you doing in your spiritual life to hear His voice?

Jesus reminds us that not everyone who calls Him Lord is part of His kingdom. Ponder on what Jesus might say to you if you came to Him and called Him Lord.

> *"Not every one who says to me, 'Lord, Lord,' shall enter the kingdom of heaven, but he who does the will of my Father who is in heaven.* On that day many will say to me, 'Lord, Lord, did we not prophesy in your name, and cast out demons in your name, and do many mighty works in your name?' And then will **I declare to them, 'I never knew you; depart from me, you evildoers.'**... *Every one then who hears these words of mine and does them* will be like a wise man who built his house upon the rock; and the rain fell, and the floods came, and the winds blew and beat upon that house, but it did not fall, because it had been founded on the rock. *And every one who hears these words of mine and does not do them* will be like a foolish man who built his house upon the sand; and the rain fell, and the floods came, and the winds blew and beat against that house, and it fell; and great was the fall of it."
>
> Matthew 7:21-27

These are sobering words that should make us resolve to make God LORD of our life. Can you imagine Christ looking at you and saying "I never knew you, depart from me you evildoer"? This breaks my heart to write it here.

When we claim we do things in Christ's name and He never sent us, we lie and deceive ourselves and others. It is not God speaking through us nor is it His work through us. We are masquerading as a believer but we are not. To be a believer we must listen to the *living* Savior within and heed His voice. We get no credit for doing our great works or speaking our great wisdom.

"In the name of the Lord" means the Lord sent you. You heard Him speak to you and are carrying out His words to you. The prophets spoke "in the name of the Lord" meaning they only spoke what God spoke through them. False prophets were those who spoke words claiming they were the Lord's but were not. We are to do all "in the name of the Lord" meaning that God's Spirit is the one speaking and doing the works. This is how Jesus lived and this is how we are to live.

> *Whatever you do, in word or deed,* **do everything in the name of the Lord Jesus**, *giving thanks to God the Father through him.*   Colossians 3:17

The kingdom of God begins with us—when we let Him be king in our life. The kingdom of God is within us when our Lord reigns as king in our life.

Living in the kingdom of God by obeying the king is a way of life that takes us out of the kingdom of this world.

> *Jesus said,* ***"Follow me."*** *But the man said, "Lord, let me first go and bury my father." But Jesus said to him, "Leave the dead to bury their own dead; but as for you, go and proclaim* **the kingdom of God**.*" Another said, "I will follow you, Lord; but let me first say farewell to those at my home." Jesus said to him, "No one who puts his hand to the plow and looks back is fit for the* **kingdom of God**.*"*   *Luke 9:59-62*

When we make God Lord of our life through Jesus Christ we change kingdoms. This requires following a new master and not continuing in the world as we did before. Our beliefs and laws dictating how we live are superceded by God's *living* voice within.

The religious leaders of Christ's day held to their Scriptures and their righteousness by doing the written word. They refused to believe in the *living* Savior, as many Christians do today. Why is this so? Religious individuals are content to be good by keeping the written law. They have no need of a *living* power within them to save them. They believe that obeying written Scriptures saves them. Let's make sure that we don't do the same and try to be good without the source of all good, God our Father.

I repeat: *Good does not come from trying to do good and avoiding evil.* Good comes only from God, who is good.

Jesus Made God Our Father LORD of His Life

Jesus didn't try to be good by avoiding evil or keeping the law. He obeyed the Spirit of God within Him. He only did what God was doing through Him and only spoke what God was speaking through Him.

Referring to Himself and His purpose, Jesus said:

> "***The Spirit of the Lord is upon me***, *because he has anointed me to preach good news to the poor. He has sent me to proclaim release to the captives and recovering of sight to the blind, to set at liberty those who are oppressed, to proclaim the acceptable year of the Lord."* Luke 4:18-19

When Jesus was tempted by Satan to obey him and not the Lord God within Him, Jesus responded with:

> *"Begone, Satan! for it is written, '**You shall worship the Lord your God and him only shall you serve.**'"*
> Matthew 4:10; Luke 4:8

Jesus rejoiced in the Holy Spirit and called God the Father, Lord.

> *In that same hour he rejoiced in the Holy Spirit and said,* **"*I thank thee, Father, Lord of heaven and earth***, *that thou hast hidden these things from the wise and understanding and revealed them to babes; yea, Father,*

for such was thy gracious will."
Luke 10:21; Matthew 11:25

In addition, when a lawyer asked Him: "Teacher, what shall I do to inherit eternal life?", Jesus responded with:

*"**You shall love the Lord your God** with all your heart, and with all your soul, and with all your strength, and with all your mind; and your neighbor as yourself."*
Luke 10:27

When the disciples asked Jesus to show them the Father, He could say:

"Have I been with you so long, and yet you do not know me, Philip? **He who has seen me has seen the Father;** *how can you say, 'Show us the Father'? Do you not believe that **I am in the Father and the Father in me?**... The words that I say to you I do not speak on my own authority; but **the Father who dwells in me does his works**. Believe me that **I am in the Father and the Father in me**; or else believe me for the sake of the works themselves."*
John 14:9-11

Jesus was displaying Father God because of His obedience to the Spirit of God within Him. He repeatedly emphasized that His actions and words were the works of His Father who dwelled in Him. He specifically stated that His words and works were not His own.

Just as Jesus made God the Father His Lord, we are to do the same.

We Are the Temple of the Living God

We are familiar with Scripture which says we are the temple of the *living* God:

> *Do you not know that **you are God's temple** and that **God's Spirit dwells in you**?*   *1 Corinthian 3:16*

> *For **we are the temple of the living God**; as God said, "I will live in them and move among them, and I will be their God, and they shall be my people."*
> *2 Corinthians 6:16*

> *Do you not know that **your body is a temple of the Holy Spirit within you, which you have from God**? You are not your own; you were bought with a price. So glorify God in your body.*   *1 Corinthians 6:19-20*

> *So then you are no longer strangers and sojourners, but you are fellow citizens with the saints and members of the household of God, built upon the foundation of the apostles and prophets, Christ Jesus himself being the cornerstone, in whom the whole structure is joined together and grows into **a holy temple in the Lord**; in whom you also are built into it for **a dwelling place of God in the Spirit**.*   *Ephesians 2:19-22*

As believers, we are the temple of the *living* God and in His temple He desires to reign. What does it mean to be the temple of the *living* God? The Scriptures above clearly state that God's Spirit dwells in us. Awesome as this sounds, this is the way God designed us—to have God resident within.

In the Old Testament, God resided in the Holy of Holies, the innermost sanctuary of the temple. Only the chief priest could go into the Holy of Holies and commune with God.

Thanks to Christ's work on the cross, the curtain into the Holy of Holies was torn open so we now can approach the throne of grace with confidence. Jesus, our chief priest, tore the curtain so we can be priests and commune with God directly in His temple within our hearts.

> *Jesus cried again with a loud voice and yielded up his spirit. And behold, **the curtain of the temple was torn in two, from top to bottom**.*
>
> Matthew 27:50-51; Mark 15:37-38

> *It was now about the sixth hour, and there was darkness over the whole land until the ninth hour, while the sun's light failed; and **the curtain of the temple was torn in two**. Then Jesus, crying with a loud voice, said, "Father, into thy hands I commit my spirit!" And having said this he breathed his last.*
>
> Luke 23:44-46

> *"This is the covenant that I will make with them after those days, says the Lord: **I will put my laws on their hearts, and write them on their minds**," then he adds, "I will remember their sins and their misdeeds no more." Where there is forgiveness of these, there is no longer any offering for sin. Therefore, brethren, since we have confidence to enter the sanctuary by the blood of Jesus, by the new and living way which he opened for us **through the curtain**, that is, through his flesh, and since we have a great priest over the house of God, let us draw near with a true heart in full assurance of faith, with our hearts sprinkled clean from an evil conscience and our bodies washed with pure water.*
>
> Hebrews 10:16-22

Where is the Holy of Holies in your temple? Where does God reside in you? Where do you look for God when you need His guidance? Where do you commune with your Father? As believers, we are the temple of the *living* God and our Holy of Holies is our heart.

Think about that for a moment. The *living* God of the universe lives within you. How could anyone turn down this offer to have the God of the universe residing in them? How can we ignore God's Spirit within by not listening and heeding His voice and His promptings?

Unfathomable! Yet, we seem to do just that. Either we do not believe that God's Spirit is in us or we are rebelling against God.

How can we do this—ignoring or rejecting the *living* God's rightful place in our life?

We do it because we are content to stay in control and enjoy the world's pleasures. In other words, we do not want a Lord and Savior within. This is pride and willful self-control.

None of us want to think that we are devaluing Christ's sacrifice for us. Yet, His sacrifice was not to just give us forgiveness of sins and a place in heaven someday. He died so that we could be alive in God's Spirit. He died so that we could be brought back to life by restoration of God's Spirit in us. Are you appropriating this marvelous gift of grace?

Even when we desire to give our life to the Lord and let Him reign, we don't make this a priority. We don't spend time to get to know Him and learn to trust His guidance from within. We mouth the words of our submission, but don't actually submit because we don't trust God enough to let Him reign in our life.

Some of us, on the other hand, try to abdicate everything to God and take no responsibility for our lives. We do this because we don't take time to develop a relationship with God to know how to work with Him to do His will.

Where is the Holy of Holies within you? It is there that the *living* God wants to commune with you. We will pursue this more in the next chapter when we discuss the role of our heart in our relationship with God and why God chooses to work in and through our heart.

God Must Be Our Lord or We Are Still Under the Law

If we do not allow God to be Lord of our life, we remain under the law. It is either grace or law but not both.

Galatians and Romans both stress this:

> ***You are severed from Christ, you who would be justified by the law; you have fallen away from grace.** For through the Spirit, by faith, we wait for the hope of righteousness...**if you are led by the spirit you are not under the law**.* *Galatians 5:4-5,18*
>
> *I do not nullify the grace of God; for if justification were through the law, then Christ died to no purpose.* *Galatians 2:21*
>
> *For sin will have no dominion over you, **since you are not under law but under grace**. What then? Are we to sin because **we are not under law but under grace**? By no means!* *Romans 6:14-15*

If we do not make God LORD, that is, allow His Spirit to rule our life, then we are not under grace. If we are not living in grace, then we are still under the law. If we are under the law, then we are not under grace.

If we are not following God's Spirit within, which is good, then the only option is to revert to the law to be good. Just like Adam and Eve, we have a choice between the Tree of Life and the Tree of Law. The Tree of the Knowledge of Good and Evil is the Tree of Law—it defines what is good and evil. The Tree of Life, on the other hand, is Christ in us. Either we live from the inside out with God, who is good, in charge, or we live from without by rules and beliefs, which define good and evil.

We have the choice to have God's Spirit reign in our life or to go it alone and stay under the laws of good and evil.

Grace is foremost submitting to God so that He can do His will in and through us. We have to do this first step of humility before we can ever hope to fulfill the great commandment of loving God with all our heart, with all our mind, and with all our strength.

God's divine influence upon our heart is a prerequisite to being a child of God and living in grace.

Chapter 3: Heart-Relationship With God

God wanting an influence on our life is not a surprise to us, but God wanting to reign in our hearts and speak to us from His throne within is threatening to many. We are trained to not listen to our heart or to trust it.

Most of us can quote the following Scripture to support our belief about the heart.

> *The heart is deceitful above all things, and desperately corrupt; who can understand it?*   *Jeremiah 17:9*

Another Scripture that convinces us to not follow our heart is Christ's admonition:

> *For out of the heart come evil thoughts, murder, adultery, fornication, theft, false witness, slander.*
> *Matthew 15:19*

Do you trust your heart? Are you willing to listen to your heart? What keeps you from trusting your heart? *What if you knew that the Spirit of God resided in your heart, would you then trust your heart?*

In this chapter we will examine why God wants to *influence our heart*. We will look at many Scripture references to our heart and what they say about the importance of our heart in believing God. There is a great difference between relying on an unredeemed heart and trusting a redeemed heart. We will see that *being a believer is more about heart believing than mind beliefs*.

Thoughts, Words, and Actions Originate In Our Heart

God has chosen to rule from our heart rather than other parts of our being because our thoughts, words, and actions originate in our heart.

Jesus clearly states that our words come from our heart and that any good or evil we do also comes from our heart.

> *The good man out of the good treasure of his heart produces good, and the evil man out of his evil treasure produces evil; for **out of the abundance of the heart his mouth speaks**.* Luke 6:45

> *For from within, **out of the heart of man**, come evil thoughts.* Mark 7:21

Later He clarifies this again when speaking to the scribes and Pharisees.

> *You brood of vipers! how can you speak good, when you are evil? For out of the abundance of the heart the mouth speaks.* Matthew 12:34

> *Jesus, knowing their thoughts, said, "Why do you **think evil in your hearts?**"* Matthew 9:4

Jesus repeatedly emphasized that the heart is the source of good and evil. He reinterpreted the written law and raised the bar by pointing to the thoughts and desires of the heart.

> *You have heard that it was said, 'You shall not commit adultery.' But I say to you that every one who looks at a woman lustfully has already committed adultery with her in his heart.* Matthew 5:27-28

Scripture tells us that God judges the heart because it is from our heart that all our words and actions flow.

It is the occupant of our heart that determines whether our works are good or evil. So trying to hide our heart behind good works will only bring judgment on us as it did the Pharisees.

> *"Woe to you, scribes and Pharisees, hypocrites! for you cleanse the outside of the cup and of the plate, but inside they are full of extortion and rapacity. You blind Pharisee! first cleanse the inside of the cup and of the plate, that the outside also may be clean. Woe to you, scribes and Pharisees, hypocrites! for you are like whitewashed tombs, which outwardly appear beautiful, but within they are full of dead men's bones and all uncleanness."* Matthew 23:25-27

Living a life where our heart is not consistent with our words and actions is living a lie and putting us into Satan's realm. Living from our heart is better than subverting it because following our heart reveals the occupant of our heart.

God wants His divine influence on our heart because the heart is the origin of our thoughts, words, and actions. If He is in charge of our heart, then our thoughts, words, and actions are automatically sanctified.

The Redeemed Heart Is Where God's Spirit Resides

Scriptures clearly teaches that *God's Spirit is in us*. Jesus Himself declared that He would send the Holy Spirit.

> *Nevertheless I tell you the truth: it is to your advantage that I go away, for if I do not go away, the Counselor will not come to you; but if I go,* ***I will send him to you****.*
> John 16:7

> *When the Counselor comes, whom I shall* ***send to you*** *from the Father, even the Spirit of truth, who proceeds from the Father, he will bear witness to me.* John 15:26

> *The Counselor, the Holy Spirit, whom the **Father will send in my name**, he will teach you all things, and bring to your remembrance all that I have said to you.*
> *John 14:26*

> *I will pray the Father, and he will give you another Counselor, to be with you for ever, even the Spirit of truth, whom the world cannot receive, because it neither sees him nor knows him; you know him, for **he dwells with you, and will be in you**.*   *John 14:16-17*

> *When the Spirit of truth comes, he will guide you into all the truth; for he will not speak on his own authority, but whatever he hears he will speak, and he will declare to you the things that are to come. He will glorify me, for he will take what is mine and declare it to you.*
> *John 16:13-14*

I don't think any of us can doubt that the Spirit of God has been made available to us. The Holy Spirit in us is part of our salvation procured for us by Christ.

The Bible shows us very clearly that God's Spirit resides in our heart.

> *God's love has been poured **into our hearts** through the Holy Spirit which has been given to us.*   *Romans 5:5*

> *But it is God who established us with you in Christ and has commissioned us; he has put his seal upon us and given us his Spirit **in our hearts** as a guarantee.*
> *2 Corinthians 1:21-22*

> *Because you are sons, God has sent the Spirit of his Son **into our hearts**, crying, "Abba! Father!" So through God you are no longer a slave but a son, and if a son, then an heir.*   *Galatians 4:6-7*

When we receive God's Spirit in our heart and submit to Him, our heart is then a redeemed heart. Out of this redeemed heart comes good because God, who is good, is in charge.

This is the redeemed heart that God refers to when He spoke about giving us a new heart.

> *A new heart I will give you, and a new spirit I will put within you; and I will take out of your flesh the heart of stone and give you a heart of flesh. And I will put my spirit within you, and cause you to walk in my statutes and be careful to observe my ordinances.*
>
> *Ezekiel 36:26-27*

God gives us a new heart with His Spirit within us that causes us to walk in His statues and observe His ordinances.

Paul acknowledges the new heart in his fellow believers at Corinth.

> *You yourselves are our letter of recommendation, **written on your hearts**, to be known and read by all men; and you show that you are a letter from Christ delivered by us, written not with ink but with the **Spirit of the living God, not on tablets of stone but on tablets of human hearts**.*
>
> *2 Corinthians 3:2-3*

The redeemed heart—the believing heart—is where the Spirit of the *living* God resides.

God doesn't want to influence our lives from without; He wants to be LORD within. He desires influence on our heart directly by being the occupant of our heart. Having God's presence within our heart and giving Him authority to influence our life is the essence of living in grace.

The Redeemed Heart Is Where We Hear God's Voice

God wants a place in our life where He can guide us. He speaks to us from within our heart. This is the *living*, present tense, voice of our *living* Lord.

We can choose to listen to this still, small voice from within or we can harden our hearts and refuse to listen.

> *Therefore, as the Holy Spirit says* **"Today, when you hear his voice, do not harden your hearts** *as in the rebellion, on the day of testing in the wilderness, where your fathers put me to the test and saw my works for forty years. Therefore I was provoked with that generation, and said,* **'They always go astray in their hearts; they have not known my ways.** *As I swore in my wrath, they shall never enter my rest.'"* **Take care, brethren, lest there be in any of you an evil, unbelieving heart, leading you to fall away from the living God.** *But exhort one another every day, as long as it is called "today," that none of you may be hardened by the deceitfulness of sin. For we share in Christ, if only we hold our first confidence firm to the end, while it is said* **"Today, when you hear his voice, do not harden your hearts** *as in the rebellion."*   Hebrews 3:7-15

In the verse above, ponder the words *"Take care, lest there be in any of you an evil, unbelieving heart, leading you to fall away from the living God."* We have a *living* God within us who desires to speak with us. Refusing to listen is unbelief and rebellion like the Israelites in the wilderness.

The writer of Hebrews repeats this again emphasizing the word *today*.

> *Again he sets a certain day, "Today," saying through David so long afterward, in the words already quoted,*

"Today, when you hear his voice, do not harden your hearts." Hebrews 4:7

Every day we have the opportunity to listen and obey or to refuse to listen and remain under the law. Grace is listening and heeding the *living* God within.

Jesus illustrates this perfectly with the parable of the sower when talking about the kingdom of God within us.

When his disciples asked him what this parable meant, he said, "To you it has been given to know the secrets of the **kingdom of God***; but for others they are in parables, so that seeing they may not see, and hearing they may not understand. Now the parable is this: The seed is the word of God. The ones along the path are those who have heard; then* **the devil comes and takes away the word from their hearts***, that they may not believe and be saved... And as for that in the good soil, they are those who,* **hearing the word, hold it fast in an honest and good heart***, and bring forth fruit with patience."*

Luke 8:9-15

God speaks to us from within and our heart hears the words He speaks. The good heart gives God His rightful place and heeds God's words planted there.

When we don't allow God to have His rightful influence on our heart, the enemy has opportunity to influence our heart. The enemy takes away the word of God from our heart by questioning us with "Did God say" just like he did with Eve in the Garden of Eden. He tempts us to question if God is speaking to us and entices us to disbelieve God.

If we do listen to God's words, Satan tries to nullify God's words by tempting us to disobey or by luring us with cares, riches, and pleasures of this life.

Scripture warns us about being led away from God by false teachings and encourages us to strengthen our heart by grace.

*Do not be led away by diverse and strange teachings; for it is well that the **heart be strengthened by grace**, not by foods, which have not benefited their adherents.*
Hebrews 13:9

Our faith is dependent on our hearing God's voice.

*So then **faith cometh by hearing, and hearing by the word of God**.*   *Romans 10:17*

The word of God referred to here is the Greek word *rhema*—the *living* words God is speaking to us today. When we hear God speak to us, we will have faith to believe and obey.

God is *alive* and desiring to communicate with us; we are the ones not listening. Our heart can hear His voice if we make the choice to submit to Him in our heart.

The Heart Understands; The Mind Interprets

Our heart is where we understand what is happening in the world around us. Our mind searches through its vast store of information to interpret what the heart knows.

In worldly terms, we call this instinct. Some call it gut sense, a hunch or our sixth sense. Whatever you want to call it, we all have these insights. Surely, you have had a sudden inspiration that came seemingly out of nowhere.

When we have given our heart to God and made Him LORD, these are inspirations from God's Spirit within. To try to rationalize these promptings from the LORD with our mind, is to become double-minded and distrusting of the occupant of our heart.

This may seem strange and even false, but Scripture says that we understand with our heart.

> For **this people's heart has grown dull**, *and their ears are heavy of hearing, and their eyes they have closed, lest they should perceive with their eyes, and hear with their ears, and* **understand with their heart**, *and turn for me to heal them.*   *Matthew 13:15; Acts 28:27*

> *Jesus said to them, "Why do you discuss the fact that you have no bread?* **Do you not yet perceive or understand? Are your hearts hardened?"**   *Mark 8:17*

Jesus didn't say their minds were dull. No, He said their hearts were dull.

Our heart is the place where we first get indications that something is disturbing us.

> *And he said to them,* **"Why are you troubled, and why do questionings rise in your hearts?"**   *Luke 24:38*

> *When Jesus perceived their questionings, he answered them,* **"Why do you question in your hearts?"**
>   *Luke 5:22*

> *Now some of the scribes were sitting there,* **questioning in their hearts**, *"Why does this man speak thus? It is blasphemy! Who can forgive sins but God alone?" And immediately Jesus, perceiving in his spirit that they thus questioned within themselves, said to them,* **"Why do you question thus in your hearts?"**   *Mark 2:6-8*

Questions about what is happening first arise in our heart. The mind then tries to make sense of what we don't understand. Our spirit sees and knows before our mind does.

Have you ever had difficulty putting what you sense in your heart into words? This is particularly true when we sense something different from what our eyes are seeing or our ears are hearing. Our heart knows, but our mind is unable to comprehend what our heart understands.

God's Spirit in our heart is speaking to us and prompting us. Learning to listen to our heart and heed its promptings is part of learning to live in grace.

We Believe With Our Heart, Not Our Mind

Our heart is where we believe God or not. It is not a matter of beliefs of the mind but a matter of believing in a *living* God within the heart.

God is in us, not out there somewhere remote from us. When we accept Jesus as our Lord, God's Spirit comes to dwell within us. Believing God is believing in Him, a *living* Lord. Believing is listening to His words and heeding His commands from within.

Believing is a heart function. We are not under the law—the written words from Scripture, but under grace—God's present tense divine influence on our heart—His reigning from within.

> *Moses writes that the man who practices the righteousness which is based on the law shall live by it. But the righteousness based on faith says, Do not say **in your heart**, "Who will ascend into heaven?" (that is, to bring Christ down) or "Who will descend into the abyss?" (that is, to bring Christ up from the dead). But what does it say? The word is near you, on your lips and **in your heart** (that is, the word of faith which we preach); because, if you confess with your lips that Jesus is Lord and **believe in your heart** that God raised him from the dead, you will be saved. For **man believes with his heart** and so is justified, and he confesses with his lips and so is saved.* Romans 10:5-10

*According to the riches of his glory he may grant you to **be strengthened with might through his Spirit in the inner man, and that Christ may dwell in your hearts through faith**; that you, being rooted and grounded in love, may have power to comprehend with all the saints what is the breadth and length and height and depth, and to know the love of Christ which surpasses knowledge, that you may be **filled with all the fullness of God**. Now to him who by **the power at work within us** is able to do far more abundantly than all that we ask or think, to him be glory.*   *Ephesians 3:16-21*

Our faith is not about beliefs, but about believing. When Jesus was asked "What must we do, to be doing the works of God?", Jesus answered, "This is the work of God that you believe in Him whom He has sent."

Our faith is all about believing in a person—not Bible knowledge and beliefs. The Pharisees had a superior knowledge of Scripture and obeyed the written word. *Head knowledge is religion. Heart believing is faith.*

Knowledge in our minds about someone is very different from *knowing* a person and believing in Him. Being a believer is more about heart believing than mind beliefs.

*"Let not your **hearts** be troubled; **believe in God, believe also in me**."*   *John 14:1*

Christ allowed God to reign supreme in His life and is a perfect reflection of God our Father. We too need to allow God to be Lord of our life and allow Him to reign in our heart. As His children, He then can do His works through us as He did through Jesus.

*That the God of our Lord Jesus Christ, the Father of glory, may give you a spirit of wisdom and revelation in the knowledge of him, having the **eyes of your hearts***

> *enlightened, that you may know what is the hope to which he has called you, what are the riches of his glorious inheritance in the saints, and what is **the immeasurable greatness of his power in us who believe**.*
> *Ephesians 1:17-19*

> *Truly, I say to you, whoever says to this mountain, Be taken up and cast into the sea, and **does not doubt in his heart, but believes** that what he says will come to pass, it will be done for him.*
> *Mark 11:23*

Faith and doubt are a function of our heart. When Jesus healed people He commended their faith with a reference to their heart.

> *Jesus turned, and seeing her he said, **"Take heart, daughter; your faith has made you well."** And instantly the woman was made well.*
> *Matthew 9:22*

> *And behold, they brought to him a paralytic, lying on his bed; and **when Jesus saw their faith** he said to the paralytic, **"Take heart, my son; your sins are forgiven."***
> *Matthew 9:2*

Repeatedly Scripture admonishes us to not lose heart which means to not lose our faith.

> *Let us not grow weary in well-doing, for in due season we shall reap, if we **do not lose heart**.*
> *Galatians 6:9*

> *He told them a parable, to the effect that they ought **always to pray and not lose heart**.*
> *Luke 18:1*

> *We **do not lose heart**. Though our outer nature is wasting away, our inner nature is being renewed every day.*
> *2 Corinthians 4:16*

Jesus often rebuked people for their unbelief and associated it with hardness of heart.

*Afterward he appeared to the eleven themselves as they sat at table; and he upbraided them for their **unbelief and hardness of heart, because they had not believed** those who saw him after he had risen.*   Mark 16:14

*And he said to them, "O foolish men, and **slow of heart to believe** all that the prophets have spoken!"*
                                                                Luke 24:25

*Now this I affirm and testify in the Lord, that you must no longer live as the Gentiles do, in the futility of their minds; they are darkened in their understanding, **alienated from the life of God** because of the ignorance that is in them, **due to their hardness of heart;** they have become callous and have given themselves up to licentiousness, greedy to practice every kind of uncleanness.*   Ephesians 4:17-19

When we receive God's Spirit in our heart, Scripture tells us that we receive the mind of Christ. We have the mind of God's Spirit.

*Now we have received not the spirit of the world, but the Spirit which is from God, that we might understand the gifts bestowed on us by God. And we impart this in words not taught by human wisdom but **taught by the Spirit**, interpreting spiritual truths to those who possess the Spirit. The unspiritual man does not receive the gifts of the Spirit of God, for they are folly to him, and he is not able to understand them because they are spiritually discerned. The spiritual man judges all things, but is himself to be judged by no one. "For who has known the mind of the Lord so as to instruct him?" But **we have the mind of Christ**.*   1 Corinthians 2:12-16

*God who searches the **hearts of men** knows what is the **mind of the Spirit**, because the Spirit intercedes for the saints according to the will of God.*   Romans 8:27

When we don't trust God's Spirit in our heart—the mind of God's Spirit—and try to assess God's promptings with our unrenewed minds, we become double-minded.

> *If any of you lacks wisdom, let him ask God, who gives to all men generously and without reproaching, and it will be given him. But **let him ask in faith, with no doubting**, for he who doubts is like a wave of the sea that is driven and tossed by the wind. For that person must not suppose that **a double-minded man, unstable in all his ways, will receive anything from the Lord**.*
>
> *James 1:5-7*

Questioning what God motivates in our heart, is unbelief. To not live from our heart is to refuse grace. This is the ultimate deceit of Satan, so he can keep control of our heart.

Believing in God's Spirit in us and heeding His influence on our heart is faith. Faith is a relationship in the heart, not a belief in the mind. Faith is living in grace.

The Heart Is Where We Obey God

Obedience is more than looking good on the outside; it is obedience from the heart. God isn't looking for adherence to the law; He is looking for willingness to follow Him from the heart.

> *But thanks be to God, that you who were once slaves of sin have become **obedient from the heart**.   Romans 6:17*
>
> ***In your hearts reverence Christ as Lord.***   *1 Peter 3:15*
>
> *This people honors me with their lips, **but their heart is far from me**; in vain do they worship me, teaching as doctrines the precepts of men. You leave the commandment of God and hold fast the tradition of men.*
>
> *Mark 7:6-8*

When we obey Scriptures making them our law, we too can leave the commandment of God and hold fast to our beliefs. Scriptures are not the criteria by which God judges us. He judges us based on whether we love Him and heed His influence upon our life today.

He is *living* and active in our lives if we will allow Him to be. When He speaks, we have the choice to listen and obey or not. If we don't listen to God's influence on our heart then we are in effect not obeying His voice.

Obedience implies we know what God's will is. To know God's will we have to hear His voice in our heart and obey what He says. Or we have to follow our heart believing He is in our heart and is motivating us.

Repeatedly in both Old and New Testaments, God is asking us to listen to His voice and obey His commandments. In the Old Testament, God made it very clear He wanted the people to listen to His voice and obey Him. This was after Moses had recorded the written laws.

> *For in the day that I brought them out of the land of Egypt, I did not speak to your fathers or command them concerning burnt offerings and sacrifices. But this command I gave them,* **'Obey my voice*,* *and I will be your God, and you shall be my people; and walk in all the way that I command you, that it may be well with you. But they* **did not obey or incline their ear, but walked in their own counsels and the stubbornness of their evil hearts***, and went backward and not forward.'*
> *Jeremiah 7:22-24*

In the New Testament, Jesus says it even more clearly. The religious people of His day refused to listen to Him and believe in Him. He tells them plainly that they don't hear because they are of their father the devil.

> *Why do you not understand what I say? It is because you cannot bear to hear my word.* ***You are of your father the devil****, and your will is to do your father's desires.... **He who is of God hears the words of God; the reason why you do not hear them is that you are not of God.***
> John 8:43-47

Our heart is where we hear God and where we obey God. Our heart is where His Spirit resides influencing us to do His will.

God Wants Willing Obedience, Not Dutiful Compliance

God desires our obedience, but not just dutiful compliance. He desires us to do what we do willingly out of love for Him.

What father wants his children to begrudgingly do something for him or do it only out of fear of consequences? God doesn't want obedience out of fear or duty. God wants an authentic heart response from us.

> *Each one must do as he has made up his mind,* ***not reluctantly or under compulsion****, for God loves a cheerful giver.* 2 Corinthians 9:7

It is not enough to just do something for God; He expects us to do it cheerfully.

When we give God our heart and allow Him to influence our heart, it is God Himself who motivates us to do His will.

> ***God is at work in you, both to will and to work for his good pleasure****. Do all things without grumbling or questioning, that you may be blameless and innocent, children of God.* Philippians 2:13-15

It is God who motivates us to will and do of His good pleasure. It is not us conjuring up motivation. Smiling on the outside while we begrudgingly do something is living a lie. Whenever our heart is not consistent with our actions and words we are living a lie and become a tool of the enemy.

Many Christians assume that what God is asking of them has to be something they don't want to do. If they want to do something they assume it is their own desire and not God's. What kind of relationship with God the Father does this imply? It implies that God is an ogre and a hard taskmaster. Those who think this don't know their Father and don't have a personal relationship with Him.

How do we know if we are doing God's will? We will never know by trying to be good and avoid evil. There are not enough laws to define good and evil yet alone the ability to do them. Only when God has His rightful place within our heart—influencing our thoughts, words, and actions—will we be doing God's will. To be sure we are doing God's will we have to give Him our life.

> *I appeal to you therefore, brethren, by the mercies of God, to* **present your bodies as a living sacrifice, holy and acceptable to God, which is your spiritual worship.** *Do not be conformed to this world but be transformed by the renewal of your mind,* **that you may prove what is the will of God***, what is good and acceptable and perfect.* Romans 12:1-2

Have you ever wondered why one man in the parable of the talents is rebuked by God? This parable reveals the relationship this man had with God and why God was so displeased.

> *Jesus proceeded to tell a parable, because he was near to Jerusalem, and because they supposed that the kingdom of God was to appear immediately. He said therefore, "A nobleman went into a far country to receive a kingdom and then return. Calling ten of his servants, he gave them ten pounds, and said to them, 'Trade with these till I come.'...When he returned,*

> *having received the kingdom, he commanded these servants, to whom he had given the money, to be called to him, that he might know what they had gained by trading.... The first came before him, saying, 'Lord, your pound has made ten pounds more.' And he said to him, 'Well done, good servant! Because you have been faithful in a very little, you shall have authority over ten cities.'... And the second came, saying, 'Lord, your pound has made five pounds.' And he said to him, 'And you are to be over five cities.'... Then another came, saying, 'Lord, here is your pound, which I kept laid away in a napkin; for **I was afraid of you, because you are a severe man; you take up what you did not lay down, and reap what you did not sow.**'... He said to him, '**I will condemn you out of your own mouth, you wicked servant**! You knew that I was a severe man, taking up what I did not lay down and reaping what I did not sow? Why then did you not put my money into the bank, and at my coming I should have collected it with interest?' And he said to those who stood by, 'Take the pound from him, and give it to him who has the ten pounds.' (And they said to him, 'Lord, he has ten pounds!') 'I tell you, that to every one who has will more be given; but from him who has not, even what he has will be taken away. But as for **these enemies of mine, who did not want me to reign over them**, bring them here and slay them before me.'"*   Luke 19:11-27

One servant thinks his master is severe and so is unwilling to risk losing the pound he has been given. The other servants invest the pound and do as the master commanded. The difference in their response is their relationship with their master.

The master is displeased with the servant who fears him and fails to obey. He says, *I will condemn you out of your own mouth, you wicked servant.*

Jesus was illustrating how our beliefs about God and our relationship with Him affect our willingness to obey His commands. This is a warning to us to check our attitudes towards God and whether we are obeying out of fear and duty or obeying willingly from our heart.

In the Matthew 25 version of the talents, the two who used the talents are commended with the words *enter into the joy of your master*. I believe God joys to have us work with Him and He, when reigning in our life, emanates this joy in and through us.

When God asks us to do something, He gives us the motivation and joy to do it. Christ Himself endured the cross having joy in His heart to do so.

> *Let us run with perseverance the race that is set before us, looking to Jesus the pioneer and perfecter of our faith, who **for the joy that was set before him endured the cross**, despising the shame, and is seated at the right hand of the throne of God.*   Hebrews 12:1-2

In the Old Testament, we note that God put His motivations in the hearts of people when He desired their cooperation. Take for example the building of the tabernacle.

> *And they came, **every one whose heart stirred him, and every one whose spirit moved him**, and brought the LORD's offering to be used for the tent of meeting, and for all its service, and for the holy garments. So they came, both men and women; all **who were of a willing heart** brought brooches and earrings and signet rings and armlets, all sorts of gold objects, every man dedicating an offering of gold to the LORD.... All the men and women, the people of Israel, **whose heart moved them to bring anything for the work** which the LORD had commanded by Moses to be done, brought it as their **freewill offering** to the LORD.... And Moses said to the people of Israel, "See, the LORD has called*

> by name Bezalel the son of Uri, son of Hur, of the tribe of Judah; and **he has filled him with the Spirit of God, with ability, with intelligence, with knowledge, and with all craftsmanship**.... And he has inspired him to teach, both him and Oholiab the son of Ahisamach of the tribe of Dan. **He has filled them with ability to do every sort of work**."... And Moses called Bezalel and Oholiab and every able **man in whose mind the LORD had put ability, every one whose heart stirred him up to come to do the work**; and they received from Moses all the **freewill offering** which the people of Israel had brought for doing the work on the sanctuary. They still kept bringing him **freewill offerings** every morning, so that all the able men who were doing every sort of task on the sanctuary came, each from the task that he was doing, and said to Moses, "The people bring much more than enough for doing the work which the LORD has commanded us to do." So Moses gave command, and word was proclaimed throughout the camp, "Let neither man nor woman do anything more for the offering for the sanctuary." So the people were restrained from bringing; for the stuff they had was sufficient to do all the work, and more.   Exodus 35:21-36:7

I like this story because it shows God's abundant supply. So much was willingly given by the people that they were instructed to stop giving. Imagine that. Do we see this today? Yes, when God is motivating the work rather than man performing good works.

When God motivates us to do something, He also gives us the ability to it.

God desires freewill offerings, not begrudging compliance. God gives us a willing heart if we allow Him to reign in us and influence our heart.

God Wants a Personal Relationship With Us

God doesn't just want influence on our hearts for the sake of control; He wants a personal relationship with us. He wants to be our Father, the one who knows what is best for us and guides us in that direction. He is the good Father that all of us desire in our hearts. He gives us His Spirit within so that we can know Him.

> *For **all who are led by the Spirit of God are sons of God**. For you did not receive the spirit of slavery to fall back into fear, but **you have received the spirit of sonship. When we cry, "Abba! Father!"** it is the Spirit himself bearing witness with our spirit that **we are children of God**, and if children, then heirs, heirs of God and fellow heirs with Christ.*   Romans 8:14-17

We are sons and daughters of God. Doesn't that seem incredible? The God of the universe wants to be our dad. When we are led by His Spirit we become His children.

What is more incredible—we become fellow heirs with Christ. Jesus as the Son of God is our brother. We are in God's family.

When we come out from under the law and live in grace we are no longer slaves of sin but sons and heirs with Christ.

> *But when the time had fully come, God sent forth his Son, born of woman, born under the law, to redeem those who were under the law, so that we might receive **adoption as sons**. And because you are sons, God has sent the Spirit of his Son into our hearts, crying, **"Abba! Father!"** So through God you are no longer a slave but a **son**, and if a **son** then an heir.*   Galatians 4:4-7

The phrase "Abba Father" is a very endearing way to address a father. Jesus used this in the Garden of Gethsemane.

> And going a little farther, he fell on the ground and prayed that, if it were possible, the hour might pass from him. And he said, "**Abba, Father**, all things are possible to thee; remove this cup from me; yet not what I will, but what thou wilt." Mark 14:35-36

When Jesus taught His disciples to pray, He began the prayer with "Father."

Throughout Scripture God is called our Father and Jesus refers to us as His brothers and sisters. When Jesus' earthly mother and brothers were asking for Him, He did not refer to them as His family, but looked over to His disciples and called them His family.

> While he was still speaking to the people, behold, his mother and his brothers stood outside, asking to speak to him. But he replied to the man who told him, "Who is my mother, and who are my brothers?" And stretching out his hand toward his disciples, he said, "**Here are my mother and my brothers! For whoever does the will of my Father in heaven is my brother, and sister, and mother.**" Matthew 12:46-50

> His mother and his brothers came to him, but they could not reach him for the crowd. And he was told, "Your mother and your brothers are standing outside, desiring to see you." But he said to them, "**My mother and my brothers are those who hear the word of God and do it.**" Luke 8:19-21

God created man for relationship with Him. Adam was God's first son. Scripture refers to Adam as God's son when it lists the linage of Christ.

> The son of Enos, the son of Seth, the son of **Adam, the son of God**. Luke 3:38

God wants us to be His children. He constantly seeks to save us from being children of Satan. This requires His Spirit to reign in us.

> *But to all who received Christ, who believed in his name, he gave power to become children of God; who were born, not of blood nor of the will of the flesh nor of the will of man, but **of God**.*   John 1:12-13

> *See what love the Father has given us, that we should be called **children of God**; and so we are. The reason why the world does not know us is that it did not know him. Beloved, **we are God's children now**.*   1 John 3:1-2

We are born of God, which means we are in a new family—God's spiritual family. We are reborn, that is, born again.

Jesus rebuked the Pharisees, who were satisfied with their laws and refused a relationship with God, as follows:

> *Why do you not understand what I say? It is because you cannot bear to hear my word. **You are of your father the devil**, and your will is to do your father's desires.*
> John 8:43-44

If we don't allow God to influence our heart, then we, like religious people of Christ's day, have the devil as our father. God wants His Spirit in our heart influencing our life and not Satan with his fleshly and worldly desires.

God is not interested in our rituals or religious practices. Too much of Christianity today has turned into traditions such as going to church, listening to sermons, singing songs, and giving an offering, and away from the intimate relationship God desires. We believe we are pleasing God with our performances but He sees it as self-righteousness.

Only when His Spirit is in charge of our life are we righteous. Our religious rituals and traditions often camouflage our lack of relationship with God and actually stand in the way of us giving up our life to Him and getting to know our Father.

I will always remember the time I was asking the Lord about what He wanted me to do. I wanted to please Him and do His will. What He explained to me has changed me and my approach to life.

God showed me Scriptures where He did great and mighty things. He showed me how He created the world and everything in it. He showed me how He defeated large armies with just a rumor and how He healed incurable diseases. Then He asked me, "Why do you think I need you to do work for me? Am I not able to do all that needs to be done?"

What He said and the way He said it made me re-evaluate the sense of urgency I had to be working for the Lord. I asked myself why I thought I was so needed. It was then that I knew in my heart that the Lord allowed me to work with Him only because He wanted to bless me and have me get to know Him better. He did not need my work. No one's salvation was hinging on my labor. He showed me that He loves everyone equally and that He reveals Himself to each and everyone.

What really struck me was His next statement. "Carolyn, I have asked you to love me. I want an intimate relationship with you. For this I need your cooperation. Love requires two. Relationship requires two. Here I need you and here it is that I want you to focus. Love me with all and everything else will take care of itself. Spend time with me and get to know me. This is eternal life."

> *This is eternal life, that they know thee the only true God, and Jesus Christ whom thou hast sent. John 17:3*

Loving the Lord with my all is my work. Believing in Him is my work. Only I can give Him my love and my faith.

God created the universe and He is perfectly capable of taking care of it without me. It is my privilege to work along side Him and to enjoy HIS work.

When people speak of a personal relationship with the Lord, I often wonder what their relationship is with the Lord. Is it one of liking Him for the blessings He gives? Surely, this is the appeal of interpreting grace as underserved blessing. What does it mean to you when you say you have a personal relationship with Christ and God the Father?

God wants a personal relationship with us—He wants us to give Him our all—to love Him with our all—to become one with His Spirit. He wants us to live in grace—His divine influence on our heart and His expression in our life.

God Desires Love—A Function of Our Heart

Relationships are about love and God asks us to love Him with all our heart, mind and soul. He loves us and desires love from us.

> *A lawyer, asked him a question, to test him. "Teacher, which is the great commandment in the law?" And he said to him, You shall **love the Lord your God with all your heart**, and with all your soul, and with all your mind. This is the great and first commandment.*
>
> *Matthew 22:35-38*

> *A lawyer stood up to put him to the test, saying, "Teacher, what shall I do to inherit eternal life?" He said to him, "What is written in the law? How do you read?" He answered, "**You shall love the Lord your God with all your heart**, and with all your soul, and with all your strength, and with all your mind; and your neighbor as yourself." And he said to him, "You have*

answered right; do this, and you will live."

Luke 10:25-28

And one of the scribes came up and heard them disputing with one another, and seeing that he answered them well, asked him, "Which commandment is the first of all?" Jesus answered, "The first is, 'Hear, O Israel: **The Lord our God, the Lord is one; and you shall love the Lord your God with all your heart***, and with all your soul, and with all your mind, and with all your strength.' The second is this, 'You shall love your neighbor as yourself.' There is no other commandment greater than these." And the scribe said to him, "You are right, Teacher; you have truly said that he is one, and there is no other but he; and to love him with all the heart, and with all the understanding, and with all the strength, and to love one's neighbor as oneself, is much more than all whole burnt offerings and sacrifices." And when Jesus saw that he answered wisely, he said to him, "You are not far from the kingdom of God." Mark 12:28-34*

When the scribes agreed with Jesus about loving the Lord our God with all our heart, Jesus said he was not far from the kingdom of God.

This man, according to Christ, was close to understanding the kingdom of God—where God reigns. He understood that God wanted control of his life.

Relationships by definition are two-way. God realizes that we are unable to love Him as long as Satan is in control of our life. God is love and therefore needs to be in charge of our heart in order for us to express love to Him. Satan cannot love.

We can go through all the motions of love—acting as if we love God, but God knows we need Him within our hearts to love because He alone is LOVE.

We know and believe the love God has for us. ***God is love****, and he who abides in love abides in God, and God abides in him.* 1 John 4:16

He who does not love does not know God; for ***God is love****.* 1 John 4:8

This is why God wants to be Lord in our heart. We are either of Satan or of God. Satan cannot love anybody. Only God, who is love, can love.

*You search the scriptures, because you think that in them you have eternal life; and it is they that bear witness to me; yet you refuse to come to me that you may have life. I do not receive glory from men. But **I know that you have not the love of God within you**. I have come in my Father's name, and you do not receive me.* John 5:39-43

Jesus is saying that even if we study our Bibles diligently we are not fulfilling what God is asking of us. He is asking us to come to Him and give Him our life. Reading about Him and what He did in history is meant to bring us to Him, not be a substitute for Him.

Who would read or reread a biography or autobiography of a person when that person is alive and present. Jesus is alive and wants us to come to Him. Our Father God is alive and wants a relationship with us. Why then do we insist on reading words from the Bible and ignoring the words He is speaking to us today?

Loving God is not about appreciating God and His works; it is about an intimate relationship with Him. Loving God is not about pleasing God, but about giving Him our life. Loving God is about our reconciliation with our Father and having a love relationship with Him.

God created man with His presence within. In the beginning man had LOVE within, but man separated from God, who is love, and as a result man has a built-in longing for love. We all desire to be loved.

We search for love in all the wrong places. We search for it in this world through family, friends, marriage, money, status, and accomplishment. Only God, who is love, can satisfy this hunger.

God asks only one thing of us: love me with all. He is asking us to give Him all our life so that He can fill us with His life—LOVE.

There Is No Other Definition for Love Than God Is Love.

Scripture clearly states that love is a fruit of God's Spirit.

> *The fruit of the Spirit is love, joy, peace, patience, kindness, goodness, faithfulness, gentleness, self-control; against such there is no law.*   *Galatians 5:22-23*

In order for us to love God as He commands, we must let Him, LOVE, express Himself in and through us. We have to make Him LORD so He can be LOVE in us. We can only receive love by surrendering to LOVE, God Himself. And we can only give love by having God, who is LOVE, reigning in our heart.

Love is not something we define; it is God Himself expressing Himself in and through us.

God knows we are unable of ourselves to love Him or to love others as He commands. As a result, we will keep searching for true love. Since He is LOVE, this means we are really searching for Him.

> *Love is of God, and he who loves is born of God and knows God.*   *1 John 4:7*

No man has ever seen God; if we love one another, God abides in us and his love is perfected in us. 1 John 4:12

There is no other definition for love than God is love. Consider the passage we often quote as the meaning of love.

Love is patient and kind; love is not jealous or boastful; it is not arrogant or rude. Love does not insist on its own way; it is not irritable or resentful; it does not rejoice at wrong, but rejoices in the right. Love bears all things, believes all things, hopes all things, endures all things. Love never ends. 1 Corinthians 13:4-8

According to this definition of love, was God kind and loving when He destroyed people in the Old Testament? Doesn't God say He is a jealous God? Doesn't God insist on His own way? We know He doesn't force us to obey, but not doing His will has consequences.

Was Christ expressing love when He called the Pharisees hypocrites, whitewashed tombs, and sons of their father the devil? There are many more examples where we might question if Christ was demonstrating love.

If we define love other than God is love, we will end up judging God and Jesus as unloving. We will be hesitant to allow God's Spirit to work in and through us. When I read Jesus' rebuke of the Pharisees, I have reservations about allowing Him to do the same through me.

God said "I AM." In the case of love, GOD IS LOVE. Our task is not to take rules from the Bible and make them laws that we try to obey—be patient, be kind, don't be jealous. These are well and good, but obeying laws puts us back under the law.

God desires for us to live in grace having His divine influence upon our heart and His life expressed through us. He is love and that is what He desires to see expressed through you and I. He is not looking for our obedience to some written law in the Bible but for His Spirit—LOVE—to flow from our heart.

In order for us to love God, we first must allow Him to give Himself to us.

> *We love, because he first loved us.*   *1 John 4:19*

Love is a relationship, not a concept, a set of rules, or Bible verses. Love is God expressed in and through us.

God Designed Us to Live in Oneness With Him

When God created man, He didn't give man a set of written laws to live by. God created man in His own image and put His Spirit within man to lead and guide man.

> *Then God said, "**Let us make man in our image, after our likeness.**"*   *Genesis 1:26*

> *The LORD God formed man of dust from the ground, and breathed into his nostrils the **breath of life**; and man became a living being.*   *Genesis 2:7*

God gave life to man by giving man His Spirit within and being one with man. All God asked was that man not separate from Him.

Since God desires a love relationship with man, He gave man the choice of being one with Him or separating from Him. Love never forces itself upon another. God, being LOVE, gives man, the object of His love, the option of loving Him and being one with Him or being separate and estranged from Him.

When man ate from the forbidden Tree of the Knowledge of Good and Evil, man chose to separate from God and as a result man died.

> *And the LORD God commanded the man, saying, "You may freely eat of every tree of the garden; but **of the tree***

> *of the knowledge of good and evil you shall not eat, for in the day that you eat of it you shall die."*
>
> *Genesis 2:16-17*

Man without God's Spirit is dead. Without God's Spirit, Satan occupies his spirit and as a result is enslaved to sin.

Man was designed to be one with God the Father and this is the purpose for Christ coming to earth to save us. Jesus made it possible for us to again have God's Spirit within and be one with our Father.

Jesus is the manifestation of God's Spirit in man. Jesus was one with God the Father.

> ***I and the Father are one.*** *John 10:30*

> *If I am not doing the works of my Father, then do not believe me; but if I do them, even though you do not believe me, believe the works, that you may know and understand that the **Father is in me and I am in the Father**.* *John 10:37-38*

> *Have I been with you so long, and yet you do not know me, Philip?* ***He who has seen me has seen the Father;*** *how can you say, 'Show us the Father?'* *John 14:9*

We too are to be manifestations of God's Spirit. We, as Christians, are to live as Christ lived relying on God's Spirit within. We are to be one with the Father through Jesus.

Jesus, in His intimate prayer with Father God just before His crucifixion, mentions our need to be one with Him and Father God.

> *"I do not pray for these only, but also for those who believe in me through their word, that they may **all be one; even as thou, Father, art in me, and I in thee, that they also may be in us**, so that the world may believe*

> *that thou hast sent me. The glory which thou hast given me I have given to them, that they may **be one even as we are one, I in them and thou in me, that they may become perfectly one**, so that the world may know that thou hast sent me and hast loved them even as thou hast loved me... I made known to them thy name, and I will make it known, **that the love with which thou hast loved me may be in them, and I in them**."*   John 17:20-26

> *And now I am no more in the world, but they are in the world, and I am coming to thee. Holy Father, keep them in thy name, which thou hast given me, that **they may be one, even as we are one**.*   John 17:11

God desires not only a relationship with us, He desires an intimate love relationship like the one He had with Jesus when He was on earth. Jesus is our example of how to live in oneness with our Father God.

Just as in marriage two become one, so in our reconciliation with our Father God do we become one—one with Christ our bridegroom and God our Father.

> *Jesus answered him, "If a man loves me, he will keep my word, and my Father will love him, and **we will come to him and make our home with him**."*   John 14:23

Being restored to oneness with God our Father is what happens when we are born again. Allowing God's Spirit within to influence our hearts and live in and through us requires oneness.

Paul said it another way:

> *He who is united to the Lord becomes one spirit with him.*   1 Corinthians 6:17

Grace is not about God controlling us; it is about an intimate relationship where we live as one being.

How can we know that we are one with God our Father? His Spirit within our heart assures us.

> *By this we know that we abide in him and he in us, because **he has given us of his own Spirit**.* 1 John 4:13
>
> *By this we know that he abides in us, **by the Spirit which he has given us**.* 1 John 3:24

What do we have to do to receive God's Spirit? Jesus tells us to ask and our Father will give us His Spirit.

> *Ask, and it will be given you; seek, and you will find; knock, and it will be opened to you. For every one who asks receives, and he who seeks finds, and to him who knocks it will be opened. What father among you, if his son asks for a fish, will instead of a fish give him a serpent; or if he asks for an egg, will give him a scorpion? If you then, who are evil, know how to give good gifts to your children, how much more will the **heavenly Father give the Holy Spirit to those who ask him!** Luke 11:9-13*

God's Spirit in us reveals Jesus as the Son of God. It is by God's Spirit working in and through us that we come to understand Jesus Christ's righteous life. God abided in Him and He in God. We too can have God abide in us and we in Him.

> *Whoever confesses that Jesus is the Son of God, **God abides in him, and he in God**. So we know and believe the love God has for us. God is love, and **he who abides in love abides in God, and God abides in him**.*
> 1 John 4:15-16

Jesus Christ is the WAY for being one with God our Father. He won this LIFE of oneness with our Father for us. We can choose to live in this grace.

When you and I can truthfully say, as Christ said, "If you see me, you have seen the Father," then we are living grace. We are allowing God's Spirit in us to have full expression.

The Heart Is Deceitful When God Is Not Reigning Within

We started this chapter with those well-known verses about the deceitfulness of our heart. I want to come back to these verses now. God is speaking about the unredeemed heart, not the redeemed heart.

> *Thus says the LORD:* "**Cursed is the man who trusts in man and makes flesh his arm, whose heart turns away from the LORD.** *He is like a shrub in the desert, and shall not see any good come. He shall dwell in the parched places of the wilderness, in an uninhabited salt land....* **Blessed is the man who trusts in the LORD, whose trust is the LORD.** *He is like a tree planted by water, that sends out its roots by the stream, and does not fear when heat comes, for its leaves remain green, and is not anxious in the year of drought, for it does not cease to bear fruit....* **The heart is deceitful above all things, and desperately corrupt; who can understand it?... I the LORD search the mind and try the heart, to give to every man according to his ways, according to the fruit of his doings.**" *Jeremiah 17:5-10*

Our hearts are deceitful when we refuse to allow God to be Lord of our life—when we refuse to allow Him to reign in our hearts and express Himself from within. In context we can see that the verse refers to the "heart that turns away from the Lord"—the unredeemed heart.

When God reigns within, we have a redeemed heart. When God reigns, the enemy—the father of deceit—cannot be there.

In the Matthew passage below, Jesus upbraids the Pharisees for their religion and lack of a heart relationship with Him.

*For the sake of your tradition, you have made void the word of God. **You hypocrites!** Well did Isaiah prophesy of you, when he said: '**This people honors me with their lips, but their heart is far from me**; in vain do they worship me, teaching as doctrines the precepts of men.'... And he called the people to him and said to them, "Hear and understand: not what goes into the mouth defiles a man, but what comes out of the mouth, this defiles a man."... Then the disciples came and said to him, "Do you know that the Pharisees were offended when they heard this saying?" He answered, "Every plant which my heavenly Father has not planted will be rooted up. Let them alone; **they are blind guides**. And if a blind man leads a blind man, both will fall into a pit."... But Peter said to him, "Explain the parable to us." And he said, "Are you also still without understanding? Do you not see that whatever goes into the mouth passes into the stomach, and so passes on?... But **what comes out of the mouth proceeds from the heart, and this defiles a man. For out of the heart come evil thoughts, murder, adultery, fornication, theft, false witness, slander**. These are what defile a man; but to eat with unwashed hands does not defile a man."*
Matthew 15:6-20

Again the passage refers to the unredeemed or uncircumcised heart where Satan has control. Therefore, what comes out of this heart is evil. When the source is evil, the result is evil.

The occupant of the redeemed heart is God's Spirit; the occupant of the unredeemed heart is Satan. We are either of God or of Satan—a sobering truth. There is no in-between state. Our heart contains either God's Spirit or Satan's.

The Pharisees were blind guides, religious leaders who were focused on keeping the laws of their Bible and rejected the *LIVING* SAVIOR in their midst. This is a warning to us so that we don't reject the *LIVING* SAVIOR within us by worshipping God with our lips when our heart is far from Him.

> *You stiff-necked people, uncircumcised in heart and ears, **you always resist the Holy Spirit**. As your fathers did, so do you.*   Acts 7:51

> *Real circumcision is a matter of the **heart**, spiritual and not literal.*   Romans 2:29

An unredeemed heart resists God's Spirit. When we continually resist God's Spirit, our heart becomes callused, hard, and impenetrable. A hard heart cannot hear God's voice and that person has no choice but to rely on the mind and its laws.

> *You must no longer live as the Gentiles do, in the futility of their minds, they are darkened in their understanding, alienated from the life of God because of the ignorance that is in them, due to their **hardness of heart**.*   Ephesians 4:17-18

> *Jesus said to them, "For your **hardness of heart** he wrote you this commandment."*   Mark 10:5

> *The Pharisees watched to see if Jesus would heal on the Sabbath. Jesus looked around at them with anger, grieved at **their hardness of heart**.*   Mark 3:5

Jesus was angered by the Pharisees' adherence to written laws, because He saw how their laws hindered them from recognizing God's Spirit within Him. These law-based religious people refused to come to Jesus because they had their righteousness in the law.

A redeemed heart has God's Spirit within. A redeemed heart is cleansed by faith in God's Spirit within.

*And God who knows the heart bore witness to them, giving them the Holy Spirit just as he did to us; and he made no distinction between us and them, but **cleansed their hearts by faith**.* Acts 15:8-9

God is willing to cleanse our hearts with His Spirit—the choice is ours.

Our Heart—Our Holy Of Holies

If God says He lives within our heart, it seems important for us to understand just where He resides within our being.

Are these references to our heart referring to our physical heart? If not our physical heart, then where within our being is God's Spirit? Does it matter where God resides within us?

Scripture tells us we are the temple of the living God and that God resides in the Holy of Holies within the temple. God did not reside in the whole temple, He resided only in the Holy of Holies.

God resides in the center-most part of the temple—in the most guarded and protected part of the building. He didn't reside in the courtyard where everyone could come. He didn't reside in the Holy place were priests attended to the showbread and candlesticks. He resided in the Holy of Holies, a place where only the High Priest could go.

The Old Testament temple is a type for the temple we become when the Lord takes residence. The question we need to answer is: *Where is our Holy of Holies where God resides within us?* Answering this question is key to understanding how to hear God's voice and follow His promptings.

I think most of us cannot say for sure exactly where the Spirit is within our being, but I believe it is important for us to understand where God's Spirit resides if we are to listen to God's voice. From where does He speak and show?

We sense that this heart is somewhere central in our being. I don't believe any of us would think of this heart as in our hand or foot. And we know from Scripture that it is not our mind or brain. So where is this heart where God speaks and shows?

The word used for heart in the New Testament is *kardia*. Strong's Concordance gives the following definition for this Greek word.

> 2588. *kardia kardia;* prolonged from a primary *kar kar* (Latin *cor*, "**heart**"); **the heart**, i.e. (figuratively) the thoughts or feelings (mind); also (by analogy) **the middle**.

The root word refers to things concerning our physical heart: cardiovascular, cardiogram, cardiologist, and cardiac arrest. This doesn't prove that it is our physical heart but it gives some indication that this place is somewhere in the middle part of the body where the heart resides.

We do know that the heart is in the central most part of our body and is the center of our life. We can be brain dead and still not be physically dead, but if our heart is dead, we are dead. So the heart, like the Holy of Holies, is the most important part of our temple.

Because our faith and living in grace are vital, we must discern where God resides in us. Where do we listen to God's voice? From where do we receive His promptings? Without knowing where to listen and obey, we will have difficulty hearing and following.

One interpretation is that God resides within our innermost being. I think of it as the part of me that will live when my physical body dies. This is the part of us that has eternal life because of God's Spirit in us. When I close my eyes and visualize what is still alive apart from my physical body, I get a sense of my innermost being.

I find that those who are content to accept God's presence within them as nebulous and mysterious are those who also have difficulty hearing His voice and relating to God our Father.

It is sad to me that so many of us have been taught to close our hearts—to guard them from deception and to protect them from hurts. Satan has been very successful in keeping us from giving our heart to anyone, including God.

It takes courage to open our hearts to the Lord and to trust Him within us. But a closed heart denies the work of Christ and keeps us from being saved and experiencing life. A closed heart eventually becomes a hardened heart, not open to LOVE.

I have found that when I listen to my heart, that is, the physical area where my heart resides, God meets me there. I believe that Scripture means tongue when it says tongue, it means feet when it mentions feet, and it means eyes when it mentions eyes? Why would it mean something other than heart when it says heart?

Even the position of the heart in the center of the body and its pivotal role in distributing blood throughout our bodies is to me an indication of its role in my temple—my Holy of Holies.

God is a loving Father who will meet us wherever we earnestly seek for Him. He will reveal to us from where He wants to communicate with us.

If you hear God's voice and heed His promptings without connecting God's throne to a physical place within you, then my emphasis on the physical heart may not be helpful to you. But if you find it hard to hear God's voice from within and to know His will for your life, then I suggest you consider what I have written and ask God to show you where He resides in you so that you can be sure you are obeying His voice and heeding His promptings.

We know our own motivations and desires by listening to our heart. When Christ redeems our heart, we know His motivations and promptings from within our heart.

I know my feelings by listening to my heart. I know love, joy, and peace as a function of my heart. These are the fruits of God's Spirit within me.

The next time you experience a desire, note where this desire registers in your consciousness. When you have a feeling of love, joy, or peace, try to discern where within yourself you sense these feelings.

If all my thoughts and actions originate in my heart, I want God's Spirit to reign in my heart and keep me from my sinful nature. I want God at the source of my being.

Hearing and obeying God's voice is not an optional aspect of our faith. Hearing and obeying is our faith. Faith is believing in our *living* Lord within. Therefore it is vital that we know from where He is speaking and prompting us.

God's influence upon our heart and our listening and obeying is living in grace. For it is by listening and obeying that we allow God to express Himself through us.

Grace is a heart function. Living in grace is a shift from mind beliefs and laws to a heart relationship.

Chapter 4: God's Expression in Our Life

Grace is God made manifest. It is God expressed through His sons and daughters as He was through Christ.

Grace is what God does in and through us, but He needs our cooperation. We first give Him our life so that He can give us His life. Then we listen and heed His voice and promptings from within.

We read about this kind of relationship with God in Scripture, yet rarely enter into it. We are too busy performing for God to rest in His work in and through us.

In this chapter I discuss the differences between believers who live in grace and people who call themselves Christians yet live under the law.

God's Works—Not Our Own Good Works

When God is in charge, our life takes a radical shift. *Instead of trying to do work for God, we surrender our life to God and experience His work through us.* We stop doing our good works and are content to allow God to express Himself through us in any way He desires. We realize that our good works produce nothing and in the end will be burned up. We are humble, knowing that only the works of God will last for eternity.

Paul understood this and acknowledges that it is the Spirit of God in him doing the work, not he himself. He knew it was the grace of God that gave him the power to preach the Gospel.

> *By the **grace of God** I am what I am and **his grace** towards me was not in vain. On the contrary I worked*

*harder than any of them though **it was not I but the grace of God which is with me**.   1 Corinthians 15:10*

*Of this gospel I was made a minister according to the **gift of God's grace which was given me by the working of his power**. To me, though I am the very least of all the saints, this **grace was given, to preach** to the Gentiles the unsearchable riches of Christ.   Ephesians 3:7-8*

*Such is the confidence that we have through Christ toward God. Not that we are competent of ourselves to claim anything as coming from us; **our competence is from God, who has made us competent to be ministers** of a new covenant, not in a written code but in the Spirit; for the written code kills, but the Spirit gives life.*
2 Corinthians 3:4-6

*To this end we always pray for you, that our God may make you worthy of his call, and may fulfil every good resolve and **work of faith by his power**, so that the name of our Lord Jesus may be glorified in you, and you in him, according to the **grace of our God and the Lord Jesus Christ**.   2 Thessalonians 1:11-12*

Today, many teachers and preachers speak words that are not from God because He is not LORD of their life. Sermons are often rehashed Bible verses learned by studying Scripture and not fresh revelation received from God. These pastors and teachers do not live in grace. They are still under the law and, as a result, they preach and teach the law—beliefs from the Bible.

Knowledge will never bring life; only God's living words bring life. God is speaking but few are listening and fewer still are willing to speak or write the words they are receiving from God.

When we live in grace we play to an audience of only one—God the Father—because we know that it is only His viewpoint that counts in His kingdom. We live in His kingdom and we serve the king only.

In Scripture we see admonitions repeatedly that good works do not earn merit with God. The only good work is God's work in and through us. This is the only lasting work and the only effective work for the kingdom of God. God reigns in His kingdom and if we consider ourselves in His kingdom then God reigns in us and desires to express Himself through us. Nothing we conjure up to do as worthwhile will produce any lasting value and most likely deceive us into thinking that we are good Christians.

Therefore, my beloved brethren, be steadfast, immovable, always ***abounding in the work of the Lord, knowing that in the Lord your labor is not in vain.***
1 Corinthians 15:58

Being a Christian is not about doing good works for God, but about letting God do His good work in and through us as Christ did. Christian means living as Christ did. Christian means submitted to the Spirit of God within us.

Many claim the name of Christ but are not of God. They are in the world's kingdom because they do not believe in God's Spirit within them and do not let God reign in their life.

Jesus confronted the Pharisees because they put themselves forward as followers of God but were just the opposite— followers of the law, the written Scriptures. They followed written words and rejected the LIVING WORD before their eyes. Christians who glory in their own works and ministries are not believers, so Jesus would say to them what He said to the Pharisees.

Woe to you, scribes and Pharisees, hypocrites! ***because you shut the kingdom of heaven against men; for you neither enter yourselves, nor allow those who would***

*enter to go in. Woe to you, scribes and Pharisees, hypocrites! for you traverse sea and land to make a single proselyte, and **when he becomes a proselyte, you make him twice as much a child of hell as yourselves**.*
Matthew 23:13-15

Sadly, much of what goes on in the name of Christ is described in Christ's words here. Christian pastors and evangelists preach the Bible instead of the LIVING WORD.

Parishioners are deceived into thinking they are saved when they are not. This is the epitome of being "a child of hell." Salvation for them is believing Christ died for their sins, attending church, studying the Bible, and giving to others. They do not make God LORD of their life.

New proselytes are not introduced to a LIVING LORD and SAVIOR. They are taught beliefs and principles from the Bible. They hear and read about grace but do not understand living in grace.

This occurs because the pastors themselves are not living in grace. They are Bible scholars living under the law and preaching this as "the way."

Jesus is THE WAY, and He showed very clearly that He lived in grace—God's divine influence on His heart and God the Father's expression through Him. He did nothing on His own but only what the Father did through Him. He did God's work, not His own.

> *Jesus said, "I am the way, and the truth, and the life; no one comes to the Father, but by me. If you had known me, you would have known my Father also; henceforth you know him and have seen him."* John 14:6-7

The Bible speaks about good works, but if we read carefully we see that the good works called for are God's work through us, not good works defined by Bible verses.

> *By grace you have been saved through faith; and this is not your own doing, it is the gift of God—**not because of works**, lest any man should boast. For we are **his workmanship, created in Christ Jesus for good works, which God prepared beforehand, that we should walk in them**.*   Ephesians 2:8-10

> *Let your light so shine before men, that they may see **your good works and give glory to your Father** who is in heaven.*   Matthew 5:16

> *Jesus answered them, "I have shown you **many good works from the Father**."*   John 10:32

Whatever we do that is truly of God is grace and brings glory to His name. Whatever is not of God is law—law that we pick up from the Bible or traditions of men. We follow church and family traditions which override the LIVING WORD of God from within.

Paul repeatedly warns believers about reverting back to works of law and away from living in grace. Although we considered this Scripture before, it is worth repeating here because we are so prone to do good works to feel good about ourselves and believe we are in good standing with God.

> *O foolish Galatians!... **Did you receive the Spirit by works of the law, or by hearing with faith?** Are you so foolish? Having begun with the Spirit, are you now **ending with the flesh?** Did you experience so many things in vain?—if it really is in vain. **Does he who supplies the Spirit to you and works miracles among you do so by works of the law, or by hearing with faith?***
> Galatians 3:1-5

I identify with the Galatians who did works to demonstrate their faith. The problem is they defined the works they did as good by the law instead of listening and doing only what God prompted them to do. They obeyed written laws instead of listening to the Spirit of God within them. We too pick up Scripture verses and make them the law by which we do our works for God.

We are not saved by works but by faith. Faith is living in grace. We know many verses that say this yet we fall into the trap of doing good works for God.

> *A man is **not justified by works of the law but through faith in Jesus Christ**, even we have believed in Christ Jesus, in order to be justified by faith in Christ, and not by works of the law, because **by works of the law shall no one be justified**.* Galatians 2:16

> *We hold that a man is **justified by faith apart from works of law**.* Romans 3:28

We believe these verses but because we lack the reality of a LIVING SAVIOR and LORD within, we continue to do works.

We claim Scripture and fall into the hands of the enemy who is very adept at tempting us to challenge God to perform for us. He did the same with Jesus and He does the same with us.

> *And the tempter came and said to Jesus, "**If you are the Son of God, command these stones to become loaves of bread**." But he answered, "It is written, 'Man shall not live by bread alone, but by every word that proceeds from the mouth of God.'" Then the devil took him to the holy city, and set him on the pinnacle of the temple, and said to him, "If you are the Son of God, throw yourself down; for it is written, '**He will give his angels charge of you**,' and '**On their hands they will bear you up, lest you strike your foot against a stone**.'" Jesus said to*

> him, "Again it is written, '**You shall not tempt the Lord your God.**'" Matthew 4:3-7

Satan loves for us to claim Scripture which then causes doubts and unbelief when God doesn't respond to our presumptuous so-called faith. Satan knows Scripture better than we do and can quote it to us as he did here with Christ. He makes it sound so spiritual. He loves to challenge our positions as sons and daughters of God.

Christ revealed what it means to live in grace and not by the law. He said He lives "by every word that proceeds from the mouth of God." Christ heard and followed only the voice of God. He didn't claim Scriptures or put God to the test by making God prove Himself. He knew His Father's voice and it is this present tense, active, and LIVING voice that He heeded. Christ didn't say "every word that proceeded (past tense) from the mouth of God," but rather "proceeds (active present tense) from the mouth of God."

God's communication is specific for the situation we find ourselves in. We need to heed the voice of God through His Spirit in our heart and not try to overcome temptation by merely quoting Scripture. The enemy can checkmate us with Scripture and we will be fooled into works of the law and away from the LIVING WORD within.

So, what about works? When we want to feel good about ourselves, we come up with justification for our works. Take the Scripture we discussed earlier.

> *What does it profit, my brethren, if a man says he has faith but has not works? Can his faith save him? If a brother or sister is ill-clad and in lack of daily food, and one of you says to them, "Go in peace, be warmed and filled," without giving them the things needed for the body, what does it profit?* ***So faith by itself, if it has no works, is dead.*** *But some one will say, "You have faith*

*and I have works." **Show me your faith apart from your works, and I by my works will show you my faith.** You believe that God is one; you do well. Even the demons believe—and shudder. Do you want to be shown, you shallow man, that **faith apart from works is barren?** Was not Abraham our father justified by works, when he offered his son Isaac upon the altar? You see that faith was active along with his works, and faith was completed by works, and the scripture was fulfilled which says, "Abraham believed God, and it was reckoned to him as righteousness"; and he was called the friend of God. **You see that a man is justified by works and not by faith alone.** And in the same way was not also Rahab the harlot justified by works when she received the messengers and sent them out another way? **For as the body apart from the spirit is dead, so faith apart from works is dead.*** James 2:14-26

This Scripture seems to justify our good works, but I want to point out several key words that make all the difference in interpreting this correctly. We know that we are saved by faith and not works. So why does this passage seem to contradict this?

The key words here are "faith apart from works." These works are the works God does through us, not the works we come up with based on obeying Scripture. God wants His throne within us and He is not dormant. *The work that God does in and through us is His work, not our good works.* They are good works because He is the originator of the work.

Abraham was justified by works and not faith alone. The key words here are "Abraham believed God." Abraham heard God's voice and obeyed. Abraham didn't come up with the idea of sacrificing his son as a good work to please God. God spoke to him and told him to do it. If Abraham had decided on his own to sacrifice Isaac, it would have been murder. If he had challenged

God by claiming some "scripture" where God promises to save His people from harm or to provide the sacrifice, he would have been tempting God and there would have been an entirely different outcome.

Faith in God results in God doing His work through us. Anything we try to do to be good is just a belief we make into a law to win favor with God. God will judge us for our good works as He does our sins. Anything that is done without faith is sin and faith only comes by hearing the active LIVING words of God. Only what God does through us is GOOD.

Often this good-works mentality is promoted by Christian organizations to encourage the volunteerism needed to support the church organization. It is often under the guise of the rewards we will receive when we get to heaven.

The rewards in heaven will be closeness to our LORD and those places will go to those who know Him and desire to be near Him—the people who realize that this is the ultimate reward. These are the ones who make this a priority in their life by living in grace.

Our good works often interfere with God's work in another's life. We try to help when we see someone going through a hard time. Our natural instinct is to help alleviate another's suffering. We believe we are acting in love.

Yet, believers know that suffering can be the catalyst that brings us to the LORD. Trials and temptations have the potential to strengthen our faith.

God asks us to believe in Him—His Spirit living within us. All God's work in our life brings us closer to Him. We need to be sure we are doing God's work in the life of another and not creating dependency on us, man. God is love and only what He does through us is love. Our loving acts are a distorted form of love—a set of beliefs rather than God, who is love, flowing through us.

Be assured that God is not looking for our good works because those will all be burned up. God is looking for His works in and through us. Our work is to believe in Him whom He sent by living as Christ did by submitting to God's Spirit.

Have you ever wondered what it means to glorify God? Living in grace, that is, doing God's work in and through us, glorifies God. Jesus said He glorified God by doing the work He was given to do.

> *I glorified thee on earth, having **accomplished the work which thou gavest me to do**.*   John 17:4

We bring God glory by letting His light shine through us.

> *Let your light so shine before men, that they may see your **good works and give glory to your Father who is in heaven**.*   Matthew 5:16

> *By this **my Father is glorified, that you bear much fruit**, and so prove to be my disciples.*   John 15:8

> *As each has received a gift, employ it for one another, as good stewards of God's varied grace: whoever speaks, as one who utters oracles of God; whoever renders service, as one who renders it by the strength which God supplies; in order that **in everything God may be glorified** through Jesus Christ. To him belong glory and dominion for ever and ever.*   1 Peter 4:10-11

> *Do you not know that your body is a temple of the Holy Spirit within you, which you have from God? You are not your own; you were bought with a price. So **glorify God in your body**.*   1 Corinthians 6:19-20

To bring God glory is to let Him display Himself through us. The Greek word for *glory* means worship and we know from Romans 12 that true spiritual worship is presenting our body a living sacrifice to God so that He can do His will through us.

*Therefore, since we are justified by faith, we have peace with God through our Lord Jesus Christ. Through him we have obtained access to this grace in which we stand, and we rejoice in our hope of **sharing the glory of God**.*

Romans 5:1-2

*To them God chose to make known how great among the Gentiles are the riches of the glory of this mystery, which is **Christ in you, the hope of glory**.*

Colossians 1:27

It is easy to do God's will when He is in charge of our life. We don't have to figure out what God's will is for our life, we submit to Him and live the adventure of what He does in and through us.

The greatest honor and glory we can give anyone is to give them our life and obey their requests lovingly and willingly.

Living under the law is trying to figure out what is good and what is evil. Living under grace is submission to the one who is good and then all that we do is good.

Living In Grace Is Doing God's Will

When we live in grace, doing God's will is a natural outcome. When we allow God to reign in our life, He is free to do His will in and through us.

He can prompt us to do His will by changing the desires of our heart to be consistent with His will. He prompts us to go to the left or to the right. He motivates us to do good, because He is the source of all good.

No longer do we search to find out what the will of God is. When we submit, we know that we will do His will. Our focus is on making Him LORD, not on trying to find out what specifically He wants from us. We live His will. We live Him.

When we ask what God's will is, we are still under the laws of good and evil rather than grace. Living in grace is allowing God's divine influence on our heart to be expressed in our life.

His will is to be LORD of our life and to be allowed to express Himself through us. His expression through us is His will.

We prove the will of God by submitting to God—presenting our bodies to Him is spiritual worship. He then does His will through us.

> *I appeal to you therefore, brethren, by the mercies of God, to **present your bodies as a living sacrifice, holy and acceptable to God, which is your spiritual worship**. Do not be conformed to this world but be transformed by the renewal of your mind, that you **may prove what is the will of God**, what is good and acceptable and perfect.*   Romans 12:1-2

We always have the choice to resist God's Spirit in us or to refuse to listen to His voice, but once we understand grace we can be more confident to trust and live from God's Spirit within us. Living in grace is God's will for us.

> *Look carefully then how you walk, not as unwise men but as wise, making the most of the time, because the days are evil. Therefore do not be foolish, but **understand what the will of the Lord is**.*
> Ephesians 5:15-17

We tend to worry about trying to ferret out what God wants in a specific situation. Our focus should be more on our submission to God's Spirit in us than our desire to have God spell out instructions. We are to be one with our Father and Christ; not subjects crying for help from afar.

We are like people who ask a friend for directions to a grocery store. Instead of supplying us with written directions, our friend tells us to follow him. Even though our friend says "follow me," we insist on written directions. Our LORD is asking us to follow Him, but we keep asking Him to tell us His will.

God's Spirit knows God's will. We have God's Spirit within us. Therefore, we have the will of God present and active within. God's Spirit within us intercedes for us according to God's will.

> *Likewise the Spirit helps us in our weakness; for we do not know how to pray as we ought, but **the Spirit himself intercedes for us** with sighs too deep for words. And he who searches the hearts of men knows what is the mind of the Spirit, **because the Spirit intercedes for the saints according to the will of God**.*   Romans 8:26-27

When I hear people praying, I can't help wondering why they are seeking a remote God's advice when they are His sons and daughters by virtue of His presence in them. We need to concentrate on who we are—children of the Most High God who loves us and makes His home within to guide and lead us.

Hopefully, this writing on grace will remind us of our inheritance and give us confidence to live as sons and daughters, entering the freedom Christ won for us.

Christ rarely prayed before He performed a healing or miracle. He had confidence that He was submitted to the Father and that the Father was doing His work through Him. Once when Jesus prayed He did so for the sake of those around Him, not because He needed to know God's will.

> *Father, I thank thee that thou hast heard me. I knew that thou hearest me always, but I have said this on account of the people standing by, that they may believe that thou*

> *didst send me. When he had said this, he cried with a loud voice, "Lazarus, come out."*   John 11:41-43

He knew the glory of God would be displayed because He was submitted to God the Father. He proceeded with confidence that He was doing God's will.

We ought to mature in our likeness to Christ so that we too are confident that God is working in and through us. This is living in grace.

God Speaks and We Hear and Obey His Voice

When we get serious about believing in Jesus and desiring to do God's will, we begin by giving God our life and submitting to Him. Our faith begins by seeking the kingdom of God—God reigning within. Everything else emanates from this first submission.

> ***Seek first his kingdom*** *and his righteousness, and all these things shall be yours as well.*   Matthew 6:33

> *Fear not, little flock, for it is **your Father's good pleasure to give you the kingdom**.*   Luke 12:32

> *Being asked by the Pharisees when the kingdom of God was coming, he answered them, "The kingdom of God is not coming with signs to be observed; nor will they say, 'Lo, here it is!' or 'There!' for behold,* ***the kingdom of God is in the midst of you.***"   Luke 17:20-21

> *Jesus answered him, "Truly, truly, I say to you,* ***unless one is born anew, he cannot see the kingdom of God....*** *Truly, truly, I say to you,* ***unless one is born of water and the Spirit, he cannot enter the kingdom of God.*** *That which is born of the flesh is flesh, and that which is born of the Spirit is spirit."*   John 3:3-6

Once God is given His rightful place in our life, we can then hear God's voice from within. When God's Spirit reigns in our heart, we have His kingdom within us. We have been reborn of God and are children of God. We can listen to our heart and follow our heart because He is the occupant of our heart. We have a redeemed heart which means God is influencing our heart and expressing Himself through us.

Scriptures show us that the disciples heard God speaking to them and prompting them.

> *While Peter was pondering the vision,* ***the Spirit said to him****, "Behold, three men are looking for you... And the* ***Spirit told me to go with them****, making no distinction."*
> *Acts 10:19; Acts 11:12*

> *And they went through the region of Phrygia and Galatia, having been* ***forbidden by the Holy Spirit to speak the word*** *in Asia. And when they had come opposite Mysia, they attempted to go into Bithynia, but the* ***Spirit of Jesus did not allow them****.*   *Acts 16:6-7*

Listening to God's voice in our heart can be scary if we don't know our Father and still see ourselves separated from Him.

When we are afraid to trust God's Spirit in our hearts, is this believing in Jesus? Is it believing in what He did for us?

Perhaps we don't listen and heed God's voice within because we still are not of God? Many still desire the things of this world and do not want to give them up. We are afraid to give up control to anyone including God our Father.

Only we know if we are committed to making God LORD of our life. Our heart knows if we have made this commitment and our heart knows if we have not.

> *By this we shall know that we are of the truth, and reassure our hearts before him whenever our hearts*

> condemn us; for God is greater than our hearts, and he knows everything. Beloved, **if our hearts do not condemn us, we have confidence before God;** and we receive from him whatever we ask, because we keep his commandments and do what pleases him.
>
> *1 John 3:19-22*

You and I know if we really mean what we say. If we have given God our heart and made Him LORD, then we can hear God's voice in our heart and need not fear being deceived.

> **He who is of God hears the words of God;** *the reason why you do not hear them is that you are not of God.*
>
> *John 8:47*

How could Jesus say it any clearer? If we are of God we can hear God's voice. It is God residing in our hearts and His Spirit speaking.

In the following discourse, Jesus made it very clear that those who are not of God are of Satan and that is why they cannot hear. To the Pharisees, Jesus said:

> *Why do you not understand what I say?* **It is because you cannot bear to hear my word. You are of your father the devil,** *and your will is to do your father's desires. He was a murderer from the beginning, and has nothing to do with the truth, because there is no truth in him. When he lies, he speaks according to his own nature, for he is a liar and the father of lies. But, because I tell the truth, you do not believe me. Which of you convicts me of sin? If I tell the truth, why do you not believe me?* **He who is of God hears the words of God; the reason why you do not hear them is that you are not of God.** *John 8:43-47*

Yes, we are either of God or of Satan, there is no middle ground. If we are of God we can hear His voice. If we are of Satan we cannot hear God's voice.

The good news is that Jesus made it possible for us to be of God. The choice is ours.

Do we believe in Jesus or do we not? Did Jesus hear God's voice? Then why are we hesitant to hear God's voice if we call ourselves Christians?

We determine who resides in our heart by our repentance and submission. We repent and ask Christ into our life and receive God's Spirit within. Then we believe that He comes and begin listening and following His voice from within.

Jesus tells us we must become as little children to enter the kingdom of God.

> *Truly, I say to you,* **whoever does not receive the kingdom of God like a child shall not enter it**.
> *Mark 10:15; Luke 18:17*

But this is difficult for individuals who trust in their abilities or in their possessions. It is especially difficult for those who seek after money, thinking it gives them power to control their lives. It is hardest for the rich man who trusts in His riches to enter the kingdom of God.

> *Jesus said to his disciples, "Truly, I say to you, it will be* **hard for a rich man to enter the kingdom of heaven**. *Again I tell you, it is easier for a camel to go through the eye of a needle than for a rich man to enter the kingdom of God."*   *Matthew 19:23-24; Luke 18:24-25*

The kingdom of God is not out there in the future. This kingdom is God reigning in our heart today. This is what it means to be saved. For without His kingdom in us, we are still in the kingdom of Satan, the ruler of this world.

Believing in Christ means to listen to our Father within and heed His voice. If we are of God why would we hesitate to engage our Father in conversation. This is the relationship our Father desires.

We are encouraged to pray and bring our requests and thanksgivings to our Father. Prayer is not a one-way communication but a two-way conversation. He hears our voice and we hear His voice.

> *Faith cometh by hearing, and hearing by the word of God.*   Romans 10:17 (KJV)

The word of God referred to here is *rhema*—God speaking to us today. Hearing God speak to us produces faith.

Hearing from God our Father is the WAY, as Jesus demonstrated when He lived on earth. The way Jesus lived in relationship with God the Father is the WAY we are to live—listening and obeying.

Living in grace is putting God on the throne of our heart and then listening to His voice and obeying.

God's Spirit In Us Teaches Us ALL Things

Remarkably, Scripture tells us that God's Spirit teaches us all things. Read the following Scriptures and rejoice that we have the ultimate instructor within.

> *And I will pray the Father, and he will give you another Counselor, to be with you for ever, even the Spirit of truth, whom the world cannot receive, because it neither sees him nor knows him; you know him, for he dwells with you, and will be in you. "I will not leave you desolate; I will come to you.... But the Counselor, **the Holy Spirit, whom the Father will send in my name, he will teach you all things**, and bring to your*

remembrance all that I have said to you."
John 14:16-18; 26

When the Spirit of truth comes, he will guide you into all the truth; *for he will not speak on his own authority, but whatever he hears he will speak, and he will declare to you the things that are to come. he will glorify me, for he will take what is mine and declare it to you. All that the Father has is mine; therefore I said that he will take what is mine and declare it to you.* John 16:13-15

I write this to you about those who would deceive you; but the anointing which you received from him abides in you, and **you have no need that any one should teach you; as his anointing teaches you about everything**, *and is true, and is no lie, just as it has taught you, abide in him.* 1 John 2:26-27

When we need help and guidance, God's Spirit within us teaches us what we need to know and what to say and do. God's Spirit is our Teacher.

God, like a good father, desires to teach us all things. This is one reason He gave us His Spirit.

What no eye has seen, nor ear heard, nor the heart of man conceived, what God has prepared for those who love him, God has revealed to us through the Spirit. For the **Spirit searches everything, even the depths of God**. *For what person knows a man's thoughts except the spirit of the man which is in him? So also no one comprehends the thoughts of God except the Spirit of God. Now we have received not the spirit of the world, but the Spirit which is from God, that we might understand the gifts bestowed on us by God. And we impart this in words not taught by human wisdom but* **taught by the Spirit**, *interpreting spiritual truths to those* *who possess the Spirit. The unspiritual man does not receive the gifts of the Spirit of God, for they are folly to him, and he is not able to understand them because they are spiritually discerned.*   *1 Corinthians 2:9-14*

Jesus was taught by God and His wisdom astounded those around Him, especially those from His home town.

On the sabbath he began to teach in the synagogue; and many who heard him were astonished, saying, "Where did this man get all this? What is the wisdom given to him? What mighty works are wrought by his hands! Is not this the carpenter, the son of Mary and brother of James and Joses and Judas and Simon, and are not his sisters here with us?" And they took offense at him.
    Mark 6:2-3; Matthew 13:53-57

Jesus' wisdom came from God the Father. He spoke only what God the Father spoke through Him. We are to do the same. We are not to look for wisdom per se; but allow Wisdom to speak in and through us.

God says that we do not need teachers because He is the teacher of teachers—the expert of experts. He is more than willing to teach us all things, including revealing Himself to us so that we can know Him.

*This is the covenant that I will make with the house of Israel after those days, says the Lord: I will put my laws into their minds, and write them on their hearts, and I will be their God, and they shall be my people. And **they shall not teach every one his fellow or every one his brother, saying, 'Know the Lord,' for all shall know me**, from the least of them to the greatest.*
    Hebrews 8:10-11

John also said we have no need for anyone to teach us.

> *The anointing which you received from him abides in you, and **you have no need that any one should teach you; as his anointing teaches you about everything**, and is true, and is no lie, just as it has taught you, abide in him.*   *1 John 2:27*

God's Spirit within us teaches us ALL things. All means all. Living in grace means we have all.

Jesus also assures us that God's Spirit will speak for us when we are brought before those who persecute us.

> *And when they bring you before the synagogues and the rulers and the authorities, do not be anxious how or what you are to answer or what you are to say; for **the Holy Spirit will teach you in that very hour what you ought to say**.*   *Luke 12:11-12*

This can mean we are confronted by spiritual leaders who are threatened by our freedom in grace. We are not to fear because God our Father, through His Spirit in us, will speak for us. Just as Jesus and Paul stood up to the religious leaders, we too may be accused of being deceived.

God's Spirit Sanctifies and Purifies

When we allow God's Spirit to become the occupant of our heart and in charge of our life, His Spirit purifies our life. God's Spirit reigning is our sanctification.

> *We ourselves were once foolish, disobedient, led astray, slaves to various passions and pleasures, passing our days in malice and envy, hated by men and hating one another; but when the goodness and loving kindness of God our Savior appeared, he saved us, not because of deeds done by us in righteousness, but in virtue of his own mercy, **by the washing of regeneration and renewal in the Holy Spirit**, which he poured out upon us*

> *richly through Jesus Christ our Savior, so that we might be **justified by his grace** and become heirs in hope of eternal life.* Titus 3:3-7

We don't cleanse ourselves or purify our lives by self-will. It is our submission to God's Spirit within our heart that sanctifies us and makes us righteous before God our Father.

When we obey God's voice and promptings, our spiritual LIFE becomes more important than our worldly life. The pleasures of this world fade in comparison to our relationship in the Spirit with God our Father. Peter speaks of sanctification by God's Spirit.

> *Peter, an apostle of Jesus Christ, To the exiles of the Dispersion in Pontus, Galatia, Cappadocia, Asia, and Bithynia, chosen and destined by God the Father and **sanctified by the Spirit for obedience to Jesus Christ** and for sprinkling with his blood: May grace and peace be multiplied to you.* 1 Peter 1:1-2

Things of this world will diminish as we experience the surpassing worth of knowing Christ. Paul notes this change from worldly to spiritual values.

> ***I count everything as loss because of the surpassing worth of knowing Christ Jesus my Lord.*** *For his sake I have suffered the loss of all things, and count them as refuse, in order that I may gain Christ and be found in him, not having a righteousness of my own, based on law, but that which is through faith in Christ, the righteousness from God that depends on faith.* Philippians 3:8-9

Paul knew that it was by faith in God's Spirit within that he gained Christ and righteousness.

God Reigning In Us Keeps Us from Sinning

Scripture makes it clear that we are under grace and not the law. When we live in grace by listening and obeying God's voice and promptings from within, we do not sin. How can God sin? We often excuse our sins because we think we cannot help it. But we have no excuse, because Jesus won our reconciliation with the Father so we, like Jesus, can be a perfect reflection of Him.

The passage we often quote to justify our sin is Paul's remorse at not being able to live the sinless life. Notice Paul's references to "I", "me", and "my."

> *I do not understand **my** own actions. For **I** do not do what **I** want, but **I** do the very thing **I** hate. Now if **I** do what **I** do not want, **I** agree that the law is good. So then it is no longer **I** that do it, but sin which dwells within **me**. For **I** know that nothing good dwells within **me**, that is, in **my** flesh. **I** can will what is right, but **I** cannot do it. For **I** do not do the good **I** want, but the evil **I** do not want is what **I** do. Now if **I** do what **I** do not want, it is no longer **I** that do it, but sin which dwells within **me**. So **I** find it to be a law that when **I** want to do right, evil lies close at hand. For **I** delight in the law of God, in **my** inmost self, but **I** see in **my** members another law at war with the law of **my** mind and making **me** captive to the law of sin which dwells in **my** members. Wretched man that **I** am! Who will deliver **me** from this body of death?*
> *Romans 7:15-24*

Paul is not trying to excuse His actions here. He is reminding the Roman Christians that they are no longer under the law but under grace. He reminds them that they are no longer living in the flesh with sinful passions aroused by the law but living in the new life of God's Spirit. In the same chapter Paul writes:

> *Likewise, my brethren,* ***you have died to the law through the body of Christ, so that you may belong to another,*** *to him who has been raised from the dead in order that we may bear fruit for God. While we were living in the flesh, our sinful passions, aroused by the law, were at work in our members to bear fruit for death.* ***But now we are discharged from the law, dead to that which held us captive, so that we serve not under the old written code but in the new life of the Spirit.***   *Romans 7:4-6*

When Christians make this excuse they do not fully understand what Christ won for them and are not living in grace.

Look at Paul's words. There are 35 references to I, me, and my in this short passage which gives us a clue to Paul's problem. Whenever we see ourselves as separated from God and under the law, we are indeed a basket case of sin. However, this is not our situation when we receive Christ's salvation and begin to live in grace with God's Spirit reigning.

If we are truly saved, we no longer can refer to ourselves as "I" but as "We." We are in oneness with God the Father and His Son Jesus Christ. God's Spirit is within us and in charge. We are saved by believing in God's Spirit within and submitting to Him. This is what Christ's dying on the cross and defeating the enemy did for us. Our faith is living in this grace.

All else is returning to the law and bemoaning our sins, defined by the law. We deny Christ when we live as if we are still under the power of Satan and sin.

Paul sees the futility of his trying to be sinless no matter how hard he tries. His statements only illustrate the necessity to live in grace and not revert to the law.

Paul's question "Who will deliver me from this body of death?" has but one answer: God's Spirit reigning within him. This is how Jesus remained sinless as a man and this is how we are to be sinless.

When we no longer live under the law but under grace, sin has no control over us.

> **Sin will have no dominion over you, since you are not under law but under grace.** Romans 6:14
>
> *We know that our old self was crucified with Him so that the sinful body might be destroyed, and* **we might no longer be enslaved to sin. For he who has died is freed from sin.** *Romans 6: 6-7*
>
> *How can we who died to sin still live in it?*
> *Romans 6:2*
>
> *Sin is not counted where there is no law.* *Romans 5:13*
>
> *Where there is no law there is no transgression.*
> *Romans 4:15*

Man believes that righteousness can be attained by avoiding evil and doing good. Man does not recognize that only God is good and it is His presence, His Spirit within as LORD, that produces good, not the elimination of evil. Everything that God created was good because He is the source of good.

Our sins are the result of our separation from God. I call this separation from God the big SIN and capitalize it to emphasize it as the SIN that God is trying to undo. I see sins as coming from this one SIN and until this big SIN is corrected, we can commit any sin.

We delude ourselves by thinking that we would not commit adultery or kill. Given the right conditions we would commit these sins unless we are living in grace, that is, under God's divine influence on our heart and His expression in our life.

When God warned Adam and Eve about the Tree of the Knowledge of Good and Evil, He didn't say they would be committing a sin if they ate of it; He said they would die.

And the LORD God commanded the man, saying, "You may freely eat of every tree of the garden; but of the tree of the knowledge of good and evil you shall not eat, for in the day that you eat of it you shall die."

Genesis 2:16-17

Why did God say they would die? Isn't this just a small disobedience that Adam and Eve should have been able to ask forgiveness for? When we disobey, don't we think of it as just a small infraction that God's love and grace will cover. We want to say we are sorry, ask for forgiveness, and be back in God graces.

So why such a big deal? Disobedience is a big deal because we separate from God when we disobey.

*And **you he made alive, when you were dead** through the trespasses and sins in which you once walked, following the course of this world, following the prince of the power of the air, the spirit that is now at work in the sons of disobedience. Among these we all once lived in the passions of our flesh, following the desires of body and mind, and so we were by nature children of wrath, like the rest of mankind.... But God, who is rich in mercy, out of the great love with which he loved us, even **when we were dead through our trespasses, made us alive together with Christ (by grace you have been saved), and raised us up with him, and made us sit with him in the heavenly places in Christ Jesus, that in the*** *coming ages he might show the immeasurable riches of his grace in kindness toward us in Christ Jesus.... For by grace you have been saved through faith; and this is not your own doing, it is the gift of God—not because of works, lest any man should boast.... For we are his workmanship, created in Christ Jesus for good works, which God prepared beforehand, that we should walk in them.*   *Ephesians 2:1-10*

When we choose to go it alone by making decisions with our mind, we commit the same sin as Adam and Eve. The result is the same—we separate ourselves from God. Separation from God is the SIN which produces all the other sins. Once we are separate from God, Satan's spirit fills the vacuum.

Alarmingly, many Christians don't believe this. They consider making independent decisions with their minds as how God made us. The mind is useful when it is subjected to the Spirit of God, but when it is under the domain of Satan it produces all kinds of fears and evils.

When we believe we are still of God, that is, God's Spirit is in us, we don't repent and turn around and renew our covenant with the LORD. At most we ask for forgiveness as if it is just a minor sin common to all. Consequently, we go on separated from God wondering why our life is filled with confusion, fears, and conduct that is not godly. We are of the world and think nothing of it. Yet, Scripture tells us that those of the world are of Satan. Yes, of Satan. Consider the following verses, which clearly state one is either of God or of the world and Satan. If of Satan then sinning; if of God then not sinning:

You know that he appeared to take away sins, and in him there is no sin. No one who abides in him sins; **no one who sins has either seen him or known him.** *Little children, let no one deceive you. He who does right is righteous, as he is righteous.* **He who commits sin is of**

> *the devil; for the devil has sinned from the beginning. The reason the Son of God appeared was to destroy the works of the devil. No one born of God commits sin; for God's nature abides in him, and he cannot sin because he is born of God.* **By this it may be seen who are the children of God, and who are the children of the devil: whoever does not do right is not of God, nor he who does not love his brother.** *1 John 3:5-10*

This is sobering. But we must come to grips with it if we are to be saved. When we are separated from God and not abiding in Him, we are in SIN and therefore sinning. When we abide in Him, that is, we are of God, we do not sin because He is reigning and it is His righteousness that is expressed.

Most Christians believe they can never be sinless. Our sins should alert us to the fact that we are separated from our LORD and therefore in the hands of the enemy. Scripture tells us that the work of Christ on the cross was to save us from sin, not just provide a way to be forgiven continually for the sins we commit.

Let's look at 1 John 3:5-10 again, this time emphasizing the good news:

> *You know that he appeared to take away sins, and in him there is no sin.* **No one who abides in him sins;** *no one who sins has either seen him or known him. Little children, let no one deceive you.* **He who does right is righteous, as he is righteous.** *He who commits sin is of the devil; for the devil has sinned from the beginning.* **The reason the Son of God appeared was to destroy the works of the devil. No one born of God commits sin; for God's nature abides in him, and he cannot sin because he is born of God. By this it may be seen who are the children of God,** *and who are the children of the devil: whoever does not do right is not of God, nor he who does not love his brother.* *1 John 3:5-10*

> *We know that any one born of God does not sin, but he who was born of God keeps him, and the evil one does not touch him.* 1 John 5:18

John repeats this message over and over. Paul too had to remind the churches that they were set free from sinning.

> *We know that our old self was crucified with him so that the sinful body might be destroyed, and we might no longer be enslaved to sin. **For he who has died is freed from sin**.* Romans 6:6-7

> *But thanks be to God, that you who were once slaves of sin have become **obedient from the heart** to the standard of teaching to which you were committed, and, **having been set free from sin, have become slaves of righteousness**.* Romans 6:17-18

> *But now that **you have been set free from sin and have become slaves of God**, the return you get is sanctification and its end, eternal life.* Romans 6:22

> *So **you also must consider yourselves dead to sin and alive to God in Christ Jesus**. Let not sin therefore reign in your mortal bodies, to make you obey their passions. Do not yield your members to sin as instruments of wickedness, but **yield yourselves to God** as men who have been brought from death to life, **and your members to God** as instruments of righteousness. **For sin will have no dominion over you, since you are not under law but under grace**.* Romans 6:11-14

We have died to sin because we have died to our old self by letting God's Spirit be our life. Paul said it correctly when he said "It is no longer I, but Christ in me." It is the life that Christ brings within and our abiding in Him that makes us righteous and prevents us from sinning. Yes, prevents us from sinning

127

because we are independent no longer but now are under the influence of God's Spirit who cannot sin.

Notice the phrases "yield yourselves to God," "slaves of God" and "obedient from the heart." This is what grace is: God's divine influence upon our heart and therefore His ability to express Himself in our lives. Therefore sin has no more control over us because we are under GRACE.

This is the wonderful news of the gospel that many of us do not understand and therefore don't appropriate. We remain in our sin—separated from God not realizing that we must repent and turn. We have to get back under God's authority, giving up our independent attempts to be self-righteous by obeying laws.

Salvation is so much more than we realize. Instead of just being a wiping away of sins we have committed, it is foremost a way of not sinning at all. That is what the above Scriptures state and Christ illustrated by His life on earth.

Living in grace is a sinless nature, letting Him express Himself through us eliminates our SIN and therefore sins.

You may be surprised to know the definition of *forgiveness*, a word that we throw around lightly.

In Strong's Greek Concordance, the Greek word for "forgiveness" is *aphesis* which means freedom.

>859. *aphesis aphesis;* from 863; **freedom**; (figuratively) pardon:—**deliverance**, forgiveness, **liberty**, remission.

>863. *aphiēmi aphiemi;* from 575 and *iēmi hiemi* (**to send; an intensive form** of *eimi eimi*, to go); **to send forth**, in various applications: cry, forgive, **forsake, lay aside, leave, let go, omit, put away, send away, remit**, suffer, **yield up**.

>575. *apo apo;* a primary particle; "off," i.e. away from something near: hereafter, ago, at, because of, before, by forth, from, in, (out) of, off, (up-)on(-ce), since, with. **In**

composition (as a prefix) it usually denotes separation,
departure, cessation, completion, reversal**, etc.

What I see in these definitions is a different meaning from what I thought for most of my Christian life. I see:

- freedom from sinning
- deliverance from sinning
- separation from sin
- departure from sinning
- cessation of sinning

Doesn't this seem impossible? Can we really be sinless? Yes, because this is what Christ won for us and God's grace provides.

We have watered down Christ's work on the cross and God's grace. Once we consider what forgiveness really means, we will see that it is exactly what Scripture says: freedom from sinning. We are predisposed to see forgiveness as an erasing of sins already committed. This was true for me and I can see that others see forgiveness only as a remedy for past sins. Few of us understand the extent of Christ's salvation. *We are free from sinning!*

Not convinced? Reread the Scriptures included here and ask God's Spirit to show you the meaning. It was hard for me to accept this definition of forgiveness of sins. It wasn't until God showed me the true meaning of His grace that I understood the completeness of my salvation through His Spirit in me and being LORD of my life.

Scripture refers to our salvation as redemption. Redemption also means cessation from sinning. So that you can make a determination for yourself, I have included the Strong's Concordance entry for *redemption*:

> 629. *apolytrōsis apolutrosis;* from a compound of 575 and 3083; **ransom in full**, i.e. figuratively **riddance**, or specially **Christian salvation:—deliverance**, redemption.

575. *apo apo;* a primary particle; "off," i.e. away from something near: hereafter, ago, at, because of, before, by forth, from, in, (out) of, off, (up-)on(-ce), since, with. **In composition (as a prefix) it usually denotes separation, departure, cessation, completion, reversal**, etc.

3083. *lytron lutron;* from 3089; something to loosen with, i.e. a redemption price (figuratively, **atonement**):—**ransom**.

We see that forgiveness and redemption indicate freedom and cessation from sinning:

- ransomed from sinning
- riddance from sinning
- salvation from sinning
- deliverance from sinning
- separation from sin
- departure from sinning
- cessation of sinning

Jesus came to save us from sinning, not just provide forgiveness for our continual sinning. He didn't leave us in bondage. He set us free.

Let's say a man bails us out of prison. Does he ransom us so that we can continue our sinful ways and return to jail or is it to give us the possibility of freedom and a better life? Christ's salvation is not just a past tense redemption, but a present tense spiritual presence to keep us from sinning.

Consider these Scriptures that emphasize our deliverance, not just our pardon:

> *He has delivered us from the dominion of darkness and transferred us to the kingdom of his beloved Son, in whom we have* **redemption** *[cessation from sinning], the forgiveness of sins.*   *Colossians 1:13-14*

> *In him we have **redemption** [cessation from sinning] through his blood, the forgiveness of our trespasses, according to the riches of his grace [divine influence upon our heart] which he lavished upon us.*
>
> Ephesians 1:7-8

In Hebrews the cessation of sinning is more clearly stated:

> *This is the covenant that I will make with them after those days, says the Lord: I will put my laws on their hearts, and write them on their minds, then he adds, "I will remember their sins and their misdeeds no more." Where there is **forgiveness** of these, there is no longer any offering for sin.*
>
> Hebrews 10:16-22

Christians emphasize that forgiveness is only a pardon for sins committed and are reluctant to admit that our salvation involves the elimination of sinning. One reason is that many Christians have a remote Savior even though they claim to have a personal Savior. To them personal means only that this remote Savior is concerned about them—not that their Savior is resident within them and in charge. LORD means that our Savior is in charge and to be in charge means Lord of our life. We have a Living Savior who is *one* with God our Father and is *one* with us.

Jesus emphasized this oneness:

> *I will pray the Father, and he will give you another Counselor, to be with you for ever, even the Spirit of truth, whom the world cannot receive, because it neither sees him nor knows him; you know him, for he dwells with you, and will be in you. "I will not leave you desolate; I will come to you. Yet a little while, and the world will see me no more, but you will see me; because I live, you will live also. **In that day you will know that I am in my Father, and you in me, and I in you.**"*
>
> John 14:16-20

> *I do not pray for these only, but also for those who believe in me through their word, that they may **all be one; even as thou, Father, art in me, and I in thee, that they also may be in us**, so that the world may believe that thou hast sent me. The glory which thou hast given me I have given to them, **that they may be one even as we are one, I in them and thou in me, that they may become perfectly one**, so that the world may know that thou hast sent me and hast loved them even as thou hast loved me.*   John 17:20-23

The Spirit that our Father sends to us as our Counselor is none other than the Spirit that God the Father and Jesus shared in oneness. Imagine the magnitude of our LORD and SAVIOR *living* within us. This is the profound significance of Christ's dying on the cross for our sin—our reconciliation with God our Father and restoration to a sinless nature—our new creation.

> *You, therefore, must be perfect, as your heavenly Father is perfect.*   Matthew 5:48

I see Christ's atonement as AT-ONE-MENT. Man was created sinless because of His oneness with God the Father. Jesus restored this sinless condition by making oneness with God our Father available to you and me. This is what it means to be born of God—living in grace. This is the GOOD NEWS!

We Love As God Loves

Because we allow God to be LORD of our life, He is able to show Himself through us and one of these glorious expressions is His *agape* LOVE.

Agape LOVE reigns in our heart when we live in grace with God's Spirit in charge of our heart.

> ***God's love*** *[agape] has been poured into our hearts through the Holy Spirit which has been given to us.*
> *Romans 5:5*
>
> *God did not give us a spirit of timidity but a spirit of power and **love** [agape] and self-control.   2 Timothy 1:7*
>
> *The fruit of the Spirit is **love** [agape]…   Galatians 5:22*

When God is one with us, we express *agape* love. God is love and this is the love He expresses when we allow Him to display Himself through us.

We all know the Scriptures commanding us to love the LORD and to love our neighbor as ourselves.

> *You shall **love** [agape] the Lord your God with all your heart, and with all your soul, and with all your mind. This is the great and first commandment. And a second is like it, You shall **love** [agape] your neighbor as yourself.   Matthew 22:37-39*

We have addressed the first part of this commandment to love God with our all—meaning we allow God to have His influence on our heart and life. This is the first commandment of love. This is equivalent to Christ's injunction to seek first the kingdom of God within. God is LOVE and we have this love only as we are submitted to God, who is LOVE.

The second commandment follows the first and cannot be disconnected from it. Often, as Christians, we try to do the second commandment that asks us to love others without first allowing LOVE to reign in our life. When we try to love others by ourselves it is but another good work of the law. We make this verse into law and try to love.

This is not what God is asking. He is asking us first to give Him our life and put Him in charge of our heart, *then* second to love others. How can we be so presumptuous as to think we can love someone without our Father who says He is LOVE.

When we live in grace we are a new creation—God is reigning in our life. So when it says to love others as ourselves it means as our new selves submitted to God, who is LOVE. We can only express *agape* love if we are one with His LOVE.

Our misinterpretation of loving others has created too many gushy Christian works that the enemy just delights in. He keeps us busy loving others and feeling good about ourselves while he deceives us into thinking we are doing these things in Christ's name. Unless we are submitted like Christ was to the Father and only did what God was doing through Him, we are not doing these works in Christ's name. They are not God's work; they are our own works.

People not of God and still of the world cannot keep the law of *agape* love. Their love is only *phileo* love which is based on customs and traditions—man-made laws—many of which are taken from Scripture.

> *I command you, to **love** [agape] one another.... If you were of the world, the **world would love** [phileo] its own; but because you are not of the world, but I chose you out of the world, therefore the world hates you.*
> *John 15:17-19*

We no longer live under the law when we live in grace, under God's influence upon our heart. We live in *agape* love, in oneness with God's Spirit, who is LOVE. Worldly people will not understand and actually hate us because we do not conform to their worldly definition of love.

Loving others is a natural expression of living in grace—allowing God who is LOVE to express Himself through us.

> *By this we know that we **love** [agape] the children of God, when we **love** [agape] God and obey his commandments.* 1 John 5:2

When Christ said to love God and our neighbor, He declares that *agape* love fulfills the law. Love fulfills the law because God, who is LOVE, fulfills His law. Living like Christ did—in submission to God the Father—is LOVE and fulfills the law.

Throughout the New Testaments, this theme is repeated.

> *Owe no one anything, except to **love** [agape] one another; for he who **loves** [agape] his neighbor has fulfilled the law. The commandments, "You shall not commit adultery, You shall not kill, You shall not steal, You shall not covet," and any other commandment, are summed up in this sentence, "You shall **love** [agape] your neighbor as yourself." **Love** [agape] does no wrong to a neighbor; therefore **love** [agape] is the fulfilling of the law.* Romans 13:8-10

> *For the whole law is fulfilled in one word, "You shall **love** [agape] your neighbor as yourself."* Galatians 5:14

> *If you really fulfil the royal law, according to the scripture, "You shall **love** [agape] your neighbor as yourself."* James 2:8

How can the whole law be fulfilled by loving our neighbor?

> *If we **love** [agape] one another, God abides in us and his **love** [agape] is perfected in us.*   *1 John 4:12*

To truly love our neighbor, we must have God, who is LOVE, in charge of our heart and life. We must be living in grace and not trying to live the law.

God not only asks us to love our neighbor but also our enemies. How is this possible? It is only possible with God, who is LOVE, in charge of our life.

> *You have heard that it was said, 'You shall **love** [agape] your neighbor and hate your enemy.' But I say to you, **Love** [agape] your enemies and pray for those who persecute you, so that you may be sons of your Father who is in heaven; for he makes his sun rise on the evil and on the good, and sends rain on the just and on the unjust. For if you **love** [agape] those who **love** [agape] you, what reward have you? Do not even the tax collectors do the same? And if you salute only your brethren, what more are you doing than others? Do not even the Gentiles do the same? You, therefore, must be perfect, as your heavenly Father is perfect.*
> *Matthew 5:43-48*

Loving our enemies is not performing nice and loving things for them. Loving our enemies is allowing God, who is LOVE, to flow through us to them. We have no idea what loving people is from God's perspective unless we stay submitted to Him. All to often, when faced with someone who persecutes or hurts us, we revert to Bible verses that we think define how we are to love instead of listening to God's Spirit in our heart and only doing what He prompts us to do. Could a strong word of rebuke be LOVE? God's *agape* love is so different from anything we imagine. Jesus' admonition at the end of this verse sums it up. Be perfect as your Father is perfect. This is only possible by being in total submission to our Father and letting Him express Himself, LOVE.

God is LOVE and when allowed to influence our heart and express Himself, He fulfills the law with Himself, LOVE. God's purpose in giving the law was to bring us back into a oneness relationship with Him. When we live in grace, there is no longer a need for the law.

When we love God with our all and allow Him to reign in our hearts, we keep all His commandments. We allow Him to express Himself through us by listening and obeying.

> *If you **love** [agape] me, you will keep my commandments.*   *John 14:15*

> *This is the **love** [agape] of God, that we keep his commandments. And his commandments are not burdensome.*   *I John 5:3*

> *This is **love** [agape], that we follow his commandments; this is the commandment, as you have heard from the beginning, that you follow love [agape].*   *2 John 6*

Jesus says that those who love Him keep His commandments and those who keep His commandments love Him. It is both. We obey His commandments by coming to Him and believing in Him; then He and the Father make their home in us and manifest themselves in and through us.

> *As the Father has loved [agape] me, so have I loved [agape] you; abide in my **love** [agape]. If you keep my commandments, **you will abide in my love** [agape], just as I have kept my Father's commandments and abide in his love [agape]. "This is my commandment, that you love [agape] one another as I have loved [agape] you."*   *John 15:9-12*

> *He who has my commandments and keeps them, he it is who loves [agape] me; and he who loves [agape] me will be loved [agape] by my Father, and I will love [agape] him and manifest myself to him.... If a man loves [agape] me, he will keep my word, and my Father will love [agape] him, and **we will come to him and make our home with him**. He who does not love [agape] me does not keep my words; and the word which you hear is not mine but the Father's who sent me.* John 14:21-24

Jesus asks us to live in grace as He did—in oneness LOVE and therefore obedience to God our Father.

John encourages us with the same words.

> *Whoever keeps his word, in him truly love [agape] for God is perfected. By this we may be sure that we are in him: he who says he abides in him ought to walk in the same way in which he walked.* 1 John 2:5-6

These Scriptures refer to our oneness with our Father. They are about walking in grace.

When these Scriptures say to "keep my commandments" and "follow my commandments" they do not refer to written laws, but to directions our Father gives us through His Spirit in our heart. We live as Jesus did in constant union with our Father in a love relationship.

> *I do as the Father has commanded me, so that the world may know that I love [agape] the Father.* John 14:31

Living in grace is all about love—love for our Father first, and then in union with our Father, who is LOVE, loving others as ourselves.

We Bear Fruit—Fruits of God's Spirit In Us

When we live in grace, we exhibit the fruits of God's Spirit in and through us as naturally as a healthy tree produces fruit. God's Spirit within us produces His fruit.

> *The fruit of the Spirit is love, joy, peace, patience, kindness, goodness, faithfulness, gentleness, self-control; against such there is no law.* Galatians 5:22-23

These fruits are first produced within us and then flow through us to others. Often we see this fruit as being there to be picked by others, but fruits such as love, joy, and peace are ours first. It is out of the abundance of these fruits within us that they then flow to others. God does not use us merely as a conduit. One who has not known love cannot flow with love. One who has not known peace cannot bring peace to another.

By ourselves we cannot produce any of these fruits. They result from our submission and oneness with our Father and Jesus Christ.

> *Abide in me, and I in you. As the branch cannot bear fruit by itself, unless it abides in the vine, neither can you, unless you abide in me. I am the vine, you are the branches. he who abides in me, and I in him, he it is that bears much fruit, for apart from me you can do nothing.... By this my Father is glorified, that you bear much fruit, and so prove to be my disciples.*
> John 15:4-8

Jesus used this illustration to emphasize our need to be united with Him and our Father in order to produce good fruit.

Our life produces either good or evil depending on who reigns in our heart—God or Satan. If God, we produce good fruit; if Satan, evil fruit.

> *No good tree bears bad fruit, nor does a bad tree bear good fruit; each tree is known by its fruit.*
> *Luke 6:43-44; Matthew 7:17-18*

> *Either make the tree good, and its fruit good; or make the tree bad, and its fruit bad; for the tree is known by its fruit.... The good man out of his good treasure brings forth good, and the evil man out of his evil treasure brings forth evil.*   *Matthew 12:33-35*

Living in grace means God is on the throne of our heart and we are heeding the words God speaks to us from within. Jesus illustrates this in His explanation of the parable of the seed sower.

> *As for that in the good soil, they are those who, hearing the word, hold it fast in an honest and good heart, and bring forth **fruit** with patience.*
> *Luke 8:15; Matthew 13:23; Mark 4:20*

When we truly believe that God reigns within us and we trust Him to influence our heart, we allow Him to exhibit the fruits of His Spirit.

We Demonstrate God's Power—Gifts of God's Spirit

When we live in grace, God demonstrates His power in and through us. When we are united with LOVE, our actions and words become God's works and not our own.

When we live in grace, we don't seek to use God or put Him to the test to prove Himself. Instead we are available to Him to do His kingdom work.

Some of us, however, want God to exhibit His power through us to prove His presence in us or to make us the spiritual ones others look up to and follow. We want to do healing and miracles or receive prophetic words for others. We seek our own glory.

Our motives are not pure unless we are living in grace and have God, who is LOVE, in charge.

> *If I speak in the tongues of men and of angels,*
> **but have not love,** *[agape]*
> *I am a noisy gong or a clanging cymbal.*
> *And if I have prophetic powers, and understand all mysteries and all knowledge, and if I have all faith, so as to remove mountains,*
> **but have not love,** *[agape]*
> *I am nothing.*
> *If I give away all I have, and if I deliver my body to be burned,*
> **but have not love,** *[agape]*
> *I gain nothing.*   *1 Corinthians 13:1-3*

God's power can only be revealed through a person who loves God above all and operates in oneness with Him. Jesus is our role model. He did only what the Father was doing through Him. He sought God the Father's glory, not His own. We, too, can display God's power and glory by allowing Him to display Himself through us.

If God chooses to speak through us then we prophesy. If God chooses to encourage someone through us then we exhibit the gift of exhortation. Whatever gift God chooses to demonstrate through us is not our prerogative, but His. These are gifts of His Spirit in us, not indications of our power. The power and glory are all His.

Immediately following the Roman 12 Scripture about presenting our bodies as a living sacrifice to prove the will of God in our life, Paul writes about gifts of God's Spirit. He admonishes us not to think of ourselves as possessing these gifts, but as having them by grace—the measure of faith God gives us to allow His work to be done through us.

> *For **by the grace given to me** I bid every one among you not to think of himself more highly than he ought to think, but to think with sober judgment, each according to the measure of faith which God has assigned him. For as in one body we have many members, and all the members do not have the same function, so we, though many, are one body in Christ, and individually members one of another. Having gifts that differ **according to the grace given to us, let us use them**: if prophecy, in proportion to our faith; if service, in our serving; he who teaches, in his teaching; he who exhorts, in his exhortation; he who contributes, in liberality; he who gives aid, with zeal; he who does acts of mercy, with cheerfulness. Let love be genuine.*   Romans 12:3-9

It is only by our faith in God's presence in us and His words and promptings from within that we can do God's will. All else is sin.

> *Whatever does not proceed from faith is sin.*
>   Romans 14:23

God motivates us from within and He speaks from within. When He speaks and motivates us, He gives us the faith to do His works.

I am alarmed when I see others trying to have gifts of God's Spirit when they have not made Him Lord of their life. This can only lead to misuse and deception. Whatever we do, great or small, without God who is LOVE, is of no value and is a deception of the enemy for us and others.

God intended us to live as Jesus did in the power of His Spirit within.

Jesus answered them, "Have faith in God. Truly, I say to you, whoever says to this mountain, 'Be taken up and cast into the sea,' and does not doubt in his heart, but believes that what he says will come to pass, it will be done for him." Mark 11:22-23

When we live submitted to our Father, He is able to do great things through us as He did through Christ. The prerequisite is LOVE in our heart. Everything we do needs to emanate from God's Spirit within our heart. This is living grace—living from LOVE.

Chapter 5: Jesus Is Grace Manifested

God gave us a clear picture of what it means to live in grace. He came to earth in His Son, Jesus Christ. Jesus is grace manifested.

Jesus Is Our Role Model for Living In Grace

Jesus came to earth to do what God the Father sent Him to do. From His example, we can learn how we are to live. What works did He do and what was God the Father's response to His Son's obedience?

Jesus repeatedly said that He did nothing but what the Father did; and said nothing but what the Father spoke.

> *Jesus said to them, "Truly, truly, I say to you,* **the Son can do nothing of his own accord, but only what he sees the Father doing;** *for whatever he does, that the Son does likewise. For the Father loves the Son, and shows him all that he himself is doing."* John 5:19-20
>
> **I can do nothing on my own authority;** *as I hear, I judge; and my judgment is just, because I seek not my own will but the will of him who sent me.* John 5:30
>
> *I have not spoken on my own authority;* **the Father who sent me has himself given me commandment what to say and what to speak.** *And I know that his commandment is eternal life. What I say, therefore, I say as the Father has bidden me.* John 12:49-50
>
> *I declare to the world what I have heard from him.... I do nothing on my own authority* **but speak thus as the**

Father taught me. And he who sent me is with me; he has not left me alone, for I always do what is pleasing to him. John 8:26-29

I do as the Father has commanded me, so that the world may know that I love the Father. John 14:31

*Do you not believe that I am in the Father and the Father in me? The words that I say to you I do not speak on my own authority; but **the Father who dwells in me does his works**. Believe me that I am in the Father and the Father in me; or else believe me for the sake of the works themselves.* John 14:10-11

*Jesus said to them, "My food is to do the will of him who sent me, and to **accomplish his work**."* John 4:34

Jesus didn't go about initiating works He wanted to do or felt needed to be done. He didn't read Scripture to pick up verses to fulfill. No, He did only what God the Father did through Him. When He spoke, He spoke only the words of His Father, not His own.

How could He do this? He could do this because He was surrendered to the Spirit of God in Him. He lived in oneness with the Father. Jesus manifested grace: God's divine influence upon His heart and God's reflection in His life. Jesus is our role model.

We, too, are to do God's works and not our own. We do this by surrender to God's Spirit within. We become one with God our Father as Jesus was.

When Jesus came to the end of His life, He could truthfully say to His Father:

*I glorified thee on earth, having **accomplished the work** which you gave me to do.* John 17:4

Jesus was able to say this because He made God the Father LORD of His life. God's Spirit within Him was His command center.

He didn't interpret the word *command* or *commandment* as some written law, but as the living active words of God from God's Spirit within Him. Commands come from the King and Christ knew that the Kingdom of God was within Him. We too, are to obey the commandments coming from our Living LORD within.

Here is what God His Father had to say about His Son:

> *This is my beloved Son,* ***with whom I am well pleased;*** *listen to him.*   *Matthew 17:5*

At Jesus' baptism, the Spirit of God descended on Him.

> *When Jesus was baptized...the heavens were opened and he saw* ***the Spirit of God descending*** *like a dove, and* ***alighting on him;*** *and lo, a voice from heaven, saying,* ***"This is my beloved Son, with whom I am well pleased."***   *Matthew 3:16-17*

I would like to hear God say this about me. Would you?

Immediately after Jesus was baptized with the Spirit of God, He is led by God's Spirit into the wilderness to be tempted by the devil.

> *Then Jesus was* ***led up by the Spirit*** *into the wilderness to be tempted by the devil.*   *Matthew 4:1*

> *The tempter came and said to him, "If you are the Son of God, command these stones to become loaves of bread." But he answered, "It is written, 'Man shall not live by bread alone, but by every word that proceeds from the mouth of God.'"*   *Matthew 4:3-4*

Jesus didn't satisfy His own needs and desires, but obeyed the present tense LIVING WORDS He heard from the mouth of God within Him. He listened to God's Spirit within.

> *Satan took him to Jerusalem, and set him on the pinnacle of the temple, and said to him, "If you are the Son of God, throw yourself down from here; for it is written, 'He will give his angels charge of you, to guard you,' and 'On their hands they will bear you up, lest you strike your foot against a stone.'" And Jesus answered him, "It is said, 'You shall not tempt the Lord your God.'"* Luke 4:9-12

Jesus kept His focus on His LIVING LORD within and didn't let Satan's quoting of Scripture deceive Him into claiming Scripture rather than obeying His LIVING LORD within.

Note what Scripture says about Jesus before and after these temptations.

> ***Jesus, full of the Holy Spirit,*** *returned from the Jordan, and was led by the Spirit for forty days in the wilderness, tempted by the devil.... And when the devil had ended every temptation, he departed from him until an opportune time. And **Jesus returned in the power of the Spirit**.* Luke 4:1-2; 13-14

Note the transformation from being "full of God's Spirit" to being "in the power of God's Spirit." Jesus, by overcoming Satan's temptations, entered into the power of God the Father.

We, too, will be led by God's Spirit into situations where we will need to believe in God's LIVING WORDS from within—where our ability to quote Scripture will not save us. We will need to hear God's voice and heed His promptings rather than engaging in a Scripture verse contest with the enemy.

Jesus Always Pointed Us to Father God

Sometimes we Christians are so focused on Jesus that we forget about our Father God.

Jesus, however, always points to Father God. Let's look at just a few of His remarks.

*If you then, who are evil, know how to give good gifts to your children, how much more will the heavenly **Father** give the Holy Spirit to those who ask him!*
Luke 11:13; Matthew 7:11

*The Counselor, the Holy Spirit, whom the **Father** will send in my name, he will teach you all things, and bring to your remembrance all that I have said to you.*
John 14:26

*Not every one who says to me, 'Lord, Lord,' shall enter the kingdom of heaven, but he who does the will of my **Father** who is in heaven.*
Matthew 7:21

*Whoever does the will of my **Father** in heaven is my brother, and sister, and mother.*
Matthew 12:50

*You heard me say to you, 'I go away, and I will come to you.' If you loved me, you would have rejoiced, because I go to the **Father**; for the **Father** is greater than I.*
John 14:28

*Jesus said to them, "If **God** were your **Father**, you would love me, for I proceeded and came forth from God; I came not of my own accord, but he sent me."*
John 8:42

*But of that day and hour no one knows, not even the angels of heaven, nor the Son, but the **Father** only.*
Matthew 24:36, Mark 13:32

*The hour is coming, and now is, when the true worshipers will worship the **Father** in spirit and truth, for such the **Father** seeks to worship him. God is spirit, and those who worship him must worship in spirit and truth.*   John 4:23-24

*No one can come to me unless the **Father** who sent me draws him.*   John 6:44

*It is written in the prophets, 'And they shall all be taught by God.' Every one who has heard and learned from the **Father** comes to me.*   John 6:45

*Jesus answered, "If I glorify myself, my glory is nothing; it is my **Father** who glorifies me, of whom you say that he is your God."*   John 8:54

*Jesus answered them, "I have shown you many good works from the **Father**."*   John 10:32

Jesus tells us to pray to God our Father rather than to Him.

*Jesus said to them, **"When you pray, say: 'Father**, hallowed be thy name. Thy kingdom come.'"*
                                     Luke 11:2; Matthew 6:9

*Again I say to you, if two of you agree on earth about anything they ask, it will be done for them **by my Father** in heaven.*   Matthew 18:19

In that day you will ask nothing of me. *Truly, truly, I say to you,* **if you ask anything of the Father, he will give it to you in my name.** *Hitherto you have asked nothing in my name; ask, and you will receive, that your joy may be full. I have said this to you in figures; the hour is coming when I shall no longer speak to you in figures but tell you plainly of the Father. In that day you will ask in my name;* **and I do not say to you that I shall**

pray the Father for you; for the Father himself loves you, because you have loved me and have believed that I came from the Father. John 16:23-27

Jesus knew it was oneness with Father God through God's Spirit within that saves us. This was His design from the beginning and is the life that Jesus lived as a man. This is living in the grace of God—His divine influence on our heart and His expression in our life.

We Are Conformed to the Image of God's Son

Wouldn't it be wonderful if we could say to God our Father at the end of our life, "I glorified thee on earth, having accomplished the work which you gave me to do." We can, if we live in grace.

Wouldn't it be wonderful to hear the words, "This is my beloved son/daughter in whom I am well pleased."

We, too, can hear these words if we follow Jesus' example of living in God's grace—God's divine influence and expression through us.

What we don't like to hear is that we will be tempted and suffer in this world like Jesus was. This is not what we expect as Christians, we think all should be untroubled once we surrender to God. Yet, it is by these temptations and trials that we see God and enter into His fullness.

Paul and John mention this fullness repeatedly.

> *For this reason I bow my knees before the Father, from whom every family in heaven and on earth is named, that according to the riches of his glory he may grant you to be **strengthened with might through his Spirit in the inner man, and that Christ may dwell in your hearts through faith;** that you, being rooted and grounded in love, may have power to comprehend with*

*all the saints what is the breadth and length and height and depth, and to know the love of Christ which surpasses knowledge, that **you may be filled with all the fulness of God**. Now to him who by **the power at work within us** is able to do far more abundantly than all that we ask or think, to him be glory in the church and in Christ Jesus to all generations, for ever and ever.*

Ephesians 3:14-21

*To all who received him, who believed in his name, he gave **power to become children of God**; who were born, not of blood nor of the will of the flesh nor of the will of man, but of God. And the Word became flesh and dwelt among us, **full of grace** and truth; we have beheld his glory, glory as of the only Son from the Father.... And **from his fulness have we all received, grace upon grace**. For the law was given through Moses; **grace** and truth came through Jesus Christ.*   *John 1:12-17*

***In him the whole fulness of deity dwells bodily, and you have come to fulness of life in him**, who is the head of all rule and authority.*   *Colossians 2:9-10*

We will be tempted and have our faith tested. We need to make this transition from having God's Spirit within to allowing God's Spirit to reign supreme within us.

This is what Scripture means when it says we are being conformed to Jesus' image.

> ***Likewise the Spirit** helps us in our weakness; for we do not know how to pray as we ought, but the Spirit himself intercedes for us with sighs too deep for words. And he who searches the hearts of men knows what is **the mind of the Spirit**, because the Spirit intercedes for the saints according to the will of God. We know that in everything God works for good with those who love him, who are*

called according to his purpose. For those whom he foreknew he also predestined **to be conformed to the image of his Son**, *in order that he might be the first-born among many brethren.* Romans 8:26-29

Jesus is the first born of many sons and daughters who are being conformed to His image. We become brothers and sisters of Jesus.

We can read this passage and miss the meaning of being conformed to Jesus' image.

Strong's Concordance defines "conformed" as:

> 4832. *symmorphos summorphos;* from 4862 and 3444; **jointly formed**, i.e. (figuratively) similar:—conformed to, fashioned like unto.

> 4862. *syn sun, soon;* a primary preposition **denoting union; with or together**, i.e. by association, companionship, process, resemblance, possession, instrumentality, addition, etc.:—beside, with. **In composition it has similar applications, including completeness.**

> 3444. *morpheæ morphe;* perhaps from the base of 3313 (through the idea of adjustment of parts); shape; figuratively, nature:—**form**.

Conformed to His image means to be formed by unity with Him or, said another way, changed by union with.

Form (*morphe*) By Union (*syn*)

The dictionary defines "conformed" in the same way. This word comes from the Latin word *conformare*:

Con (together)

***Formare* (to form)**

This is not imitation of another where we try to emulate Jesus' behaviors. This is taking on the likeness of Jesus by becoming one with God the Father as Jesus did. We are changed into His likeness from the inside out as we submit to God's Spirit within us.

Christ is formed in us by our unity—oneness—with God the Father. Just as Jesus did nothing but what the Father did through Him, likewise we live in grace and allow God's Spirit expression through our life. We change into Christ's likeness by letting God reign in our life.

Paul understood this oneness when he said the following:

> *For I through the law died to the law, that I might live to God. I have been crucified with Christ; it is no longer I who live, but **Christ who lives in me**; and the life I now live in the flesh I live by faith in the Son of God, who loved me and gave himself for me. I do not nullify the **grace** of God; for if justification were through the law, then Christ died to no purpose.*   Galatians 2:19-21

> *By the **grace** of God I am what I am, and his **grace** toward me was not in vain. On the contrary, I worked harder than any of them, though it was **not I, but the grace of God which is with me**.*   1 Corinthians 15:10

Let us not get caught up in our desire to please God by doing works for Him and thereby putting ourselves back under works of the law. Our salvation and commendation from our Father are based on grace not laws.

God our Father wants a relationship with us in which we listen to His voice within and not follow written laws. The law was written to bring us to Christ and, by believing in Christ, reconcile us to God our Father. Christ in all His words and actions points us to God our Father. Christ epitomizes living in grace. He is the perfect reflection of God from within.

When we live in grace we become the sons and daughters of the living God. How amazing!

*God sent forth his Son, born of woman, born under the law, to redeem those who were under the law, so that **we might receive adoption as sons**. And because you are sons, God has sent the Spirit of his Son into our hearts, crying, "Abba! Father!" So through God you are no longer a slave but a son, and if a son then an heir.*
Galatians 4:4-7

*The law was our custodian until Christ came, that we might be justified by faith. But now that faith has come, we are no longer under a custodian; for **in Christ Jesus you are all sons of God**, through faith. For as many of you as were baptized into Christ have put on Christ.*
Galatians 3:24-27

***He destined us in love to be his sons** through Jesus Christ, according to the purpose of his will, to the praise of **his glorious grace** which he freely bestowed on us in the Beloved. In him we have redemption through his blood, the forgiveness of our trespasses, **according to the riches of his grace which he lavished upon us**.*
Ephesians 1:5-8

***All who are led by the Spirit of God are sons of God.** For you did not receive the Spirit of slavery to fall back into fear, **but you have received the Spirit of sonship**. When we cry, "Abba! Father!" it is the Spirit himself bearing witness with our Spirit **that we are children of God**.*   *Romans 8:14-16*

*Beloved, **we are God's children now**.*   *1 John 3:2*

We are sons and daughters of God our Father and we are brothers and sisters of our Lord Jesus Christ.

When Jesus was told His earthly mother and brothers wanted to see Him, He responded:

> *Jesus was told, "Your mother and your brothers are standing outside, desiring to see you." But he said to them, "**My mother and my brothers are those who hear the word of God and do it.**"*   Luke 8:20-21

> *A crowd was sitting about him; and they said to him, "Your mother and your brothers are outside, asking for you." And he replied, "Who are my mother and my brothers?" And looking around on those who sat about him, he said, "**Here are my mother and my brothers! Whoever does the will of God is my brother, and sister, and mother.**"*   Mark 3:32-35

This scene is repeated in Matthew, Mark, and Luke to make sure we don't miss the significance of these words.

We are in a new family. We are sons and daughters of our Heavenly Father. To live in grace is to put our allegiance in this family. We are to give our life to our Father and be conformed to our Brother, Jesus.

> *We see Jesus, who for a little while was made lower than the angels, crowned with glory and honor because of the suffering of death, so that **by the grace of God** he might taste death for every one. For it was fitting that he, for whom and by whom all things exist, **in bringing many sons to glory**, should make the pioneer of their salvation perfect through suffering. For he who sanctifies and those who are sanctified have all one origin. That is why he is not ashamed **to call them brethren**.*
>   Hebrews 2:9-11

Jesus is the pioneer of our faith and He is not ashamed to call us His brothers and sisters. We are God's sons and daughters.

Christ Set Us Free—Free from Law and Sin

When I read that Christ had set me free, I asked myself, "free from what?" Is it freedom from the punishment I deserve for my sins and rebellion from God? Is it freedom from Satan? Is it freedom from sinning? Is it freedom from the bondages of the law?

Let's look at Scriptures that explain our freedom in Christ.

We are free from the law:

For freedom Christ has set us free; stand fast therefore, and do not submit again to a yoke of slavery. Now I, Paul, say to you that if you receive circumcision [a law], *Christ will be of no advantage to you. I testify again to every man who receives circumcision* [because it is a law] *that he is bound to keep the whole law. You are severed from Christ, you who would be justified by the law;* **you have fallen away from grace.** *Galatians 5:1-4*

We are free from sin and death and our flesh:

There is therefore now no condemnation for those who are in Christ Jesus. For the law of **the Spirit of life in Christ Jesus has set me free from the law of sin and death.** *For God has done what the law, weakened by the flesh, could not do: sending his own Son in the likeness of sinful flesh and for sin, he condemned sin in the flesh, in order that the just requirement of the law might be fulfilled* **in us, who walk not according to the flesh but according to the Spirit.** *For those who live according to the flesh set their minds on the things of the flesh, but those who live according to the Spirit set their minds on the things of the Spirit.* **To set the mind on the flesh is death, but to set the mind on the Spirit is life and peace.** *For the mind that is set on the flesh is hostile to God; it*

> does not submit to God's law, indeed it cannot; and those who are in the flesh cannot please God. But **you are not in the flesh, you are in the Spirit, if in fact the Spirit of God dwells in you.** Any one who does not have the Spirit of Christ does not belong to him.
>
> Romans 8:1-9

We are free from our old self and sin:

> *We know that our **old self was crucified** with him so that the sinful body might be destroyed, and we might **no longer be enslaved to sin**. For he who has died is **freed from sin**. But if we have died with Christ, we believe that we shall also live with him. For we know that Christ being raised from the dead will never die again; death no longer has dominion over him. The death he died he died to sin, once for all, but the life he lives he lives to God. So **you also must consider yourselves dead to sin and alive to God in Christ Jesus**. Let not sin therefore reign in your mortal bodies, to make you obey their passions. Do not yield your members to sin as instruments of wickedness, but **yield yourselves to God as men who have been brought from death to life, and your members to God as instruments of righteousness. For sin will have no dominion over you, since you are not under law but under grace**. What then? Are we to sin because we are not under law but under grace? By no means! Do you not know that if you yield yourselves to any one as obedient slaves, **you are slaves of the one whom you obey, either of sin, which leads to death, or of obedience, which leads to righteousness?** But thanks be to God, that **you who were once slaves of sin have become obedient from the heart** to the standard of teaching to which you were committed, and, **having been set free from sin, have become slaves of righteousness**.... The end of those things is death. But*

> *now that **you have been set free from sin and have become slaves of God, the return you get is sanctification and its end, eternal life**. For the wages of sin is death, but the free gift of God is eternal life in Christ Jesus our Lord.*   Romans 6:6-23

We are free from the law and the slavery of sin and death because we are servants of God! We are slaves of God and slaves of righteousness. Living in grace is choosing to be a voluntary servant of God.

Your first reaction may be to think freedom is freedom from sins you commit, but this is not what is written here. It says we are set free from sin and that we are no longer to sin.

> *"If you continue in my word, you are truly my disciples, and you will know the truth, and **the truth will make you free**."…"Truly, truly, I say to you, **every one who commits sin is a slave to sin**.… So if the Son makes you free, you will be free indeed."*   John 8:31-36

We are no longer a slave to sin, we are freed from sinning. We, like Christ, have the Spirit of God in us and have become slaves of God.

Christ paid for our past sins and now we live by grace which is God's influence upon our heart and His expression in our life. We are free from sinning because we have made God the master of our life and He does not sin. We are no longer separated from God but have Him reigning in our heart. We have this freedom because of God's presence and authority over our life.

> ***Live as free men**, yet without using your freedom as a pretext for evil; but **live as servants of God**. 1 Peter 2:16*

Christ made this possible by paying the price for our waywardness and sinning. Christ made us free but we must enter into this freedom and not remain in slavery to sin. We have to allow God's Spirit to reign in our life. We must live in GRACE—God's divine influence upon our heart and His expression in and through our life.

Grace Explains What It Means to Believe In Jesus

Jesus was sent to pay our debt of sin, but He also came to show us how to live by being led by God's Spirit. Jesus came to show us how to live in grace—under God's divine influence—and how to live in oneness with our Father God.

The work of God is to believe in Jesus whom Father God sent. Jesus walked in grace and asked us to follow Him. Jesus is the Way. He did not say look at the works I did and do them. He said live as I lived—submitted to God the Father. This is the way to do God's will. The word "follow" in the Greek has a sense of union implied in the definition.

> 190. *akoloutheō akoloutheo;* from 1 (as a particle of **union**) and *keleuthos keleuthos* (a road); properly, **to be in the same way with**, i.e. to accompany (specially, as a disciple):— follow, reach.

We are to walk in union with our Lord.

As Christians, we glibly claim that we believe in Jesus, but do we really understand what it means to believe in Jesus? We recite this in the creeds, but do we really know what it means to believe in Him?

Does it mean we believe He died for our sins? Does it mean we believe the words that He spoke as written in the Bible? What does believing in Jesus really mean?

Believing in Jesus is more than believing in the cross and His resurrection. It is more than believing that He existed and did marvelous works. It is more than reading and studying His words.

Jesus is the LIVING WORD made flesh. He is God incarnate, that is, God in the flesh.

> *In the beginning was the Word, and the Word was with God, and the **Word was God**. He was in the beginning with God; all things were made through him, and without him was not anything made that was made. In him was life, and the life was the light of men.... But to all who received him, who believed in his name, he gave power to become children of God; who were born, not of blood nor of the will of the flesh nor of the will of man, but of God. And **the Word became flesh** and dwelt among us, **full of grace** and truth; we have beheld his glory, glory as of the only Son from the Father.... And **from his fulness have we all received, grace upon grace**.* John 1:1-16

When He asks us to believe in Him, He is asking us to receive His Spirit, which is one with God's Spirit. He is asking us to follow Him, that is, follow His example of giving His life to God the Father and letting God's Spirit live through Him.

Jesus is not asking us to believe in facts about Him, but in God's Spirit within and to live from this source. Jesus always pointed to His oneness relationship with God the Father.

> *Believe me that **I am in the Father and the Father in me**; or else believe me for the sake of the works themselves.* John 14:11

> *If I am not doing the works of my Father, then do not believe me; but if I do them, even though you do not believe me, believe the works, that you may know and understand that the **Father is in me and I am in the Father**.* John 10:37-38

When Jesus is asked what it takes to be doing the works of God, He told them to believe in Him and follow His example.

> They said to him, "What must we do, to be doing the works of God?" Jesus answered them, **"This is the work of God, that you believe in him whom he has sent."**
> John 6:28-29

Believing in Christ is the work of God.

Later in this same passage, Jesus tells them exactly what it means to believe in Him and follow His example.

> *I have come down from heaven,* **not to do my own will, but the will of him who sent me.** John 6:38

Jesus only spoke the words of God and only did the works of God. He did God's will, not His own. God's objective in our life is that we live like Jesus—living under His divine influence and reflecting His life from within.

> *Now the Lord is the Spirit, and where the Spirit of the Lord is, there is freedom. And we all, with unveiled face, beholding the glory of the Lord, are being changed into his likeness from one degree of glory to another; for this comes from the Lord who is the Spirit.*
> 2 Corinthians 3:17-18

Believing in Jesus is believing that He saved us from our SIN—separation from God. He reconciled us to our Father. Our part is to embrace this relationship of God's Spirit within and live like Jesus did, doing only what God said and did through Him. He was one with the Father and we too are to be one with God's Spirit in us.

How do we do this? We repent and yield our life to God. We humbly ask Him to set up His kingdom within us and let Him reign in our hearts. We then begin to listen and follow God's Spirit within.

Grace is believing in Jesus and living the same way He did. Grace is God's divine influence upon our heart and His expression in our life.

Consequences of Not Living In Grace

Grace is a gift from God. We have the choice to receive His gift and live in grace or not. When we choose to live in grace, we gain LIFE. When we choose to disregard grace, there are consequences.

If we don't live in grace, we remain under the law taking from the Tree of the Knowledge of Good and Evil. We worship written words rather than the LIVING WORD. We do our good works and have no need to listen and obey the LIVING LORD. We pitch our tent at the cross for forgiveness of sins and fail to realize we have a resurrected LIVING SAVIOR and LORD. We have a religion no different from any other religion, with brick-and-mortar temples and written words. We remain in the world and look no different from nonbelievers who control their actions to look good on the outside. Without God's Spirit reigning in our life, we are of the world.

When we try to live in grace, but cling to our worldly life, enticements draw us away from the LIVING GOD.

God warns us that we cannot serve two masters.

> *No one can serve two masters; for either he will hate the one and love the other, or **he will be devoted to the one and despise the other**. You cannot serve God and mammon.*   *Matthew 6:24*

> *For **where your treasure is, there will your heart be also**.*   *Luke 12:34*

Our heart is either focused on God's Spirit within or on the worries, riches, and pleasures of this world without.

Mammon is a god of this world. This world revolves around money and the possessions it can buy. God warns us that a love of money can lead us away from our faith.

> *There is great gain in godliness with contentment; for we brought nothing into the world, and we cannot take anything out of the world; but if we have food and clothing, with these we shall be content. But **those who desire to be rich fall into temptation, into a snare,** into many senseless and hurtful desires that plunge men into ruin and destruction. For **the love of money is the root of all evils; it is through this craving that some have wandered away from the faith** and pierced their hearts with many pangs. But as for you, man of God, shun all this; aim at righteousness, godliness, faith, love, steadfastness, gentleness.*   1 Timothy 6:6-11

The pursuit of money tempts us to violate the Spirit of God within. When we seek after riches, we are prone to exploit others and justify it as business acumen. God sees and judges our greed.

> ***Come now, you rich***, *weep and howl for the miseries that are coming upon you. Your riches have rotted and your garments are moth-eaten. Your gold and silver have rusted, and their rust will be evidence against you and will eat your flesh like fire. You have laid up treasure for the last days. Behold, **the wages of the laborers who mowed your fields, which you kept back by fraud, cry out; and the cries of the harvesters have reached the ears of the Lord of hosts.** You have lived on the earth in luxury and in pleasure; you have fattened your hearts in a day of slaughter. You have condemned, you have killed the righteous man; he does not resist you.*   James 5:1-6

God also warns us about straying from our faith by participating in the pleasures of this world.

> *They count it **pleasure** to revel in the daytime. They are blots and blemishes, reveling in their **dissipation, carousing** with you. They have **eyes full of adultery, insatiable for sin**. They entice unsteady souls. They have **hearts trained in greed**. Accursed children! **Forsaking the right way they have gone astray**; they have followed the way of Balaam, the son of Beor, who **loved gain from wrongdoing**, but was rebuked for his own transgression; a dumb ass spoke with human voice and restrained the prophet's madness.*   *2 Peter 2:13-16*

Scripture here refers to those who have known the way but have gone astray. They have been sucked back into the world, and as a result lost their salvation. They have ignored God's Spirit within them and have succumbed to the enticements without. They have failed to live in grace.

Peter assures us that we have all we need to live a life of holiness if we become partakers of God's divine nature, that is, if we live in grace under God's divine influence.

> *May **grace** and peace be multiplied to you in the knowledge of God and of Jesus our Lord. **His divine power has granted to us all things that pertain to life and godliness**, through the knowledge of him who called us to his own glory and excellence, by which he has granted to us his precious and very great promises, that through these you may escape from the corruption that is in the world because of passion, **and become partakers of the divine nature**.*   *2 Peter 1:2-4*

In subsequent verses, Peter describes how those who continually suppress God's Spirit within eventually commit the unforgivable sin.

Sinning Against God's Spirit—The Unforgivable Sin

Some Christians believe that they cannot lose their salvation, and I would like to believe this too. However, Scripture does not validate this. In fact, Scripture shows us that Christians can lose their faith.

> *For if, after they have escaped the defilements of the world through the knowledge of our Lord and Savior Jesus Christ, they are again entangled in them and overpowered, the last state has become worse for them than the first. For it would have been better for them never to have known the way of righteousness than after knowing it to turn back from the holy commandment delivered to them.* 2 Peter 2:20-21

There are very sobering words in Scripture about those who outrage God's Spirit.

> *For **if we sin deliberately after receiving the knowledge of the truth, there no longer remains a sacrifice for sins**, but a fearful prospect of judgment, and a fury of fire which will consume the adversaries. A man who has violated the law of Moses dies without mercy at the testimony of two or three witnesses. **How much worse punishment do you think will be deserved by the man who has spurned the Son of God**, and profaned the blood of the covenant by which he was sanctified, and **outraged the Spirit of grace?*** Hebrews 10:26-29

God has given us the power to choose Him or to choose the way of darkness, which is love of this world and the things in this world. God gave us the power to choose and will never revoke it because He desires a love relationship with us. Love can never be attained without the object of His love having the choice to respond or not.

With this power of choice, we choose our destiny. We can choose to give God our life and love Him with our all. We can believe that God's Spirit reigns in our heart and give Him permission to influence our life and express Himself through us. We can acknowledge God's Spirit within us or we can refuse His Spirit.

God is forever wooing us and reaching out to us. We are the ones that can turn our backs on God.

We are admonished not to grieve or quench God's Spirit.

> *Do not **grieve the Holy Spirit of God**, in whom you were sealed for the day of redemption.*   Ephesians 4:30
>
> *Do not **quench the Spirit**.*   *1 Thessalonians 5:19*

I interpret this to mean that we are to allow God's Spirit influence and expression in and through our life. We are not to resist God's Spirit by clinging to written words. We are to listen and heed His LIVING WORDS from within our heart. We are not to censor God's expression through us but allow Him full access to our life.

God is love, but we can choose to deliberately violate God's Spirit within us and ignore the grace Christ won for us.

Once we experience grace and then choose to violate God's Spirit by hardening our hearts to His voice and promptings, we are not saved because it is only by God's Spirit in us that we are saved. It is the living God within us that saves us—it is our obedience to His voice and promptings. When we choose to harden our hearts to God's voice, we choose by default to make Satan, the destroyer, the one we follow.

I read the Scriptures about the unforgivable sin and wondered if I had committed this sin?

> *"Truly, I say to you, all sins will be forgiven the sons of men, and whatever blasphemies they utter; but **whoever***

> *blasphemes against the Holy Spirit never has forgiveness, but is guilty of an eternal sin"—for they had said, "He has an unclean Spirit."*   Mark 3:28-30
>
> *And every one who speaks a word against the Son of man will be forgiven; but **he who blasphemes against the Holy Spirit will not be forgiven**.*   Luke 12:10

What does it mean to blaspheme against the Holy Spirit? Why can we speak against Jesus and be forgiven but when we blaspheme against the Holy Spirit we cannot be forgiven?

I wondered why God would treat some sin as unforgivable. In light of what we have been discussing, I believe that blasphemy against the Holy Spirit is calling the Holy Spirit evil and of Satan, therefore refusing to listen and obey God's Spirit.

God is most concerned about the big SIN, that is, separation from Him. This SIN produces all other sins. Rejecting God's Spirit is separating ourselves from God permanently. There is no other way to be saved. If we close this door, there is no way to be redeemed because we have chosen to reject God Himself as LORD of our life. We choose to go it alone and have only an external God, like all other religions have, and a God who cannot save us. We worship Him with our lips but our heart is far from Him. We remain in our SIN, separated from God.

Rejecting God's Spirit within us is not a minor infraction; it is choosing death rather than life. When we fall away after we have received God's Spirit and heard His LIVING WORDS from within, we show contempt for Christ and His salvation. To do so is to make a choice for which there is no forgiveness.

> ***It is impossible to restore again to repentance*** *those who have once been enlightened, who have tasted the heavenly gift, and have become partakers of the Holy Spirit, and have tasted the goodness of the word [rhema] of God and the powers of the age to come, if they then*

> *commit apostasy, since **they crucify the Son of God on their own account and hold him up to contempt.***
> *Hebrews 6:4-6*

Apostasy means to fall away. I cannot imagine leaving the LORD now that I have heard His precious LIVING WORDS—His *rhema*—but apparently there are those who can know God in this intimate way and still fall away. This is sobering and an added incentive to live in grace and not reject our LIVING LORD within.

Most of us need not fear the unforgivable sin, because it requires rebellion against God and His influence on our life. Some of us want God in our life; we just don't know how to enter the life Christ won for us. We don't know how to walk in God's Spirit. We may even have been taught to fear listening to God's voice.

In these cases, God is continually beckoning us to enter into the salvation He offers and to experience His wonderful gift of grace. Repentance is the key, making God LORD of our life—the divine influence of our life. It involves wanting to know Him in intimate relationship—a oneness that makes us holy and sinless because He is holy and sinless.

Eternal Life Now—Knowing God and Jesus Christ

When we live in grace, we live life as God does. Let me say that another way. When we live in grace, we allow God to live His life in and through us. This is eternal life.

> *He who sows to the Spirit will from the Spirit reap eternal life.* *Galatians 6:8*

We are living with the *eternal Spirit of the LIVING God* within. We are one with the Spirit of God. He lives in us as He lived in and through Jesus when He walked on this earth. This is our heritage—eternal life now.

> *Now that you have been set free from sin and have become slaves of God, the return you get is sanctification and its end, **eternal life**. For the wages of sin is death, but the free gift of God is **eternal life** in Christ Jesus our Lord.*   Romans 6:22-23

It is our submission to God's divine influence that leads to eternal life. The Spirit of God in us sanctifies us out of this world of flesh into God's kingdom. Slaves of God means submission to His will—a change of ownership.

In Jesus' intimate communion with our Father just before His crucifixion, He defined eternal life for us.

> ***This is eternal life, that they know thee the only true God, and Jesus Christ whom thou hast sent.***   John 17:3

He defines it as *knowing* God and Jesus. This knowing is the intimate oneness of two people. Jesus goes on in this same discussion to describe how we are one with Him and He is one with our Father.

> *I do not pray for these only, but also for those who believe in me through their word, **that they may all be one; even as thou, Father, art in me, and I in thee, that they also may be in us**, so that the world may believe that thou hast sent me. The glory which thou hast given me I have given to them, **that they may be one even as we are one, I in them and thou in me, that they may become perfectly one**, so that the world may know that thou hast sent me and hast loved them even as thou hast loved me.*   John 17:20-23

God's Spirit within us and our submission to His influence from within, manifests the life of Christ in us—the intimate oneness He had with God our Father.

Jesus describes how He lived eternal life while in the flesh:

> *I have not spoken on my own authority; the Father who sent me has himself given me commandment what to say and what to speak. And I know that **his commandment is eternal life**. What I say, therefore, I say as the Father has bidden me.* John 12:49-50

John, in his epistle, defines this oneness as abiding in the Son and the Father:

> *If what you heard from the beginning abides in you, **then you will abide in the Son and in the Father. And this is what he has promised us, eternal life.*** 1 John 2:24-25

We all know the Bible verse about God so loving the world that He sent His only Son, but do we see and comprehend the reference to eternal life.

> *For God so loved the world that he gave his only Son, that whoever believes in him should not perish but have **eternal life**.* John 3:16

Formerly I interpreted Scriptures that mentioned eternal life as meaning heaven some day. It never dawned on me that eternal life started when I received the eternal Spirit of the LIVING God within.

I interpreted the kingdom of God the same way—thinking about heaven someday rather than the kingdom of God being within me when I allow God to reign in my heart. Now I know that living in grace is to have eternal life now—knowing God and Jesus Christ intimately within. The kingdom of God is wherever God reigns.

When a man asked Jesus what He had to do to inherit eternal life, Jesus responded by speaking about the kingdom of God and telling the man to follow Him. This is such an important message that Matthew, Mark and Luke record this conversation between Jesus and this ruler.

*And a ruler asked him, "Good Teacher, **what shall I do to inherit eternal life?**" And Jesus said to him, "Why do you call me good? No one is good but God alone. You know the commandments: 'Do not commit adultery, Do not kill, Do not steal, Do not bear false witness, Honor your father and mother.'" And he said, "All these I have observed from my youth." And when Jesus heard it, he said to him, "One thing you still lack. Sell all that you have and distribute to the poor, and you will have treasure in heaven; and come, **follow me**." But when he heard this he became sad, for he was very rich. Jesus looking at him said, "How hard it is for those who have riches to enter the **kingdom of God**! For it is easier for a camel to go through the eye of a needle than for a rich man to enter the **kingdom of God**." Those who heard it said, "Then who can be saved?" But he said, "What is impossible with men is possible with God."*
          Luke 18:18-27; Matthew 19:16-26; Mark 10:17-27

We can have eternal life now if we are willing to follow Jesus' example of allowing God to work in and through us.

Jesus repeats this message to those who thought searching and knowing Scripture would give them eternal life.

*You search the scriptures, because you think that in them you have **eternal life**; and it is they that bear witness to me; yet **you refuse to come to me that you may have life**.*   John 5:39-40

He makes it very clear that He is the only Way to eternal life. This message is emphasized over and over.

*For this is the will of my Father, that every one who sees the Son and believes in him **should have eternal life**.*
          John 6:40

*He who believes in the Son of God has the testimony in himself. He who does not believe God has made him a liar, because he has not believed in the testimony that God has borne to his Son. This is the testimony, that **God gave us eternal life, and this life is in his Son. He who has the Son has life; he who has not the Son of God has not life.** I write this to you who believe in the name of the Son of God, that **you may know that you have eternal life**.*   *1 John 5:10-13*

*Truly, truly, I say to you, **He who hears my word and believes him who sent me, has eternal life**; he does not come into judgment, but has passed from death to life.*
         John 5:24

*For he whom God has sent utters the words of God, for it is not by measure that he gives the Spirit; the Father loves the Son, and has given all things into his hand. **He who believes in the Son has eternal life; he who does not obey the Son shall not see life**.*   *John 3:34-36*

*My sheep hear my voice, and I know them, and they follow me; and **I give them eternal life**.... I and the Father are one.*   *John 10:27-30*

God living in and through us is eternal life and we can have this life now by living in grace. When we allow God to have His influence on our heart and His expression in our lives, we experience eternal life—God's life now.

Kingdom of God—Heaven

In 1998, as I was starting this walk of faith, I would constantly ask the Lord to show me where He wanted me to minister to others. At that time, I was deriving my meaning and purpose from giving to others. This belief was so engrained in me that God had a hard time getting me to live grace.

I do not ordinarily write poetry, but the Lord gave me a poem to teach me the importance of my relationship with Him in contrast to the good works I desired to do for Him. God showed me that if I believe I have to perform good works to please Him, I will not enjoy heaven because these good works are not needed there.

I Checked Out Of Heaven Today

I checked out of heaven today
Couldn't find any reason to stay
No disease, no poverty, or decay
No need to preach or pray
Nothing to do, nothing to say
Everyone seemed to be okay
Alone in God's presence each and every day
I hadn't learned to live this way

Carolyn Bardsley
1998

With this poem, God showed me that I need to rest in my completeness in Him. I don't need to please Him with my works, but stay in oneness with Him. I realized that I was so wanting to do good works that I ignored His presence in me. He showed me that if I ignore His kingdom here on earth, I would check out of heaven. He showed me that He didn't need my works here and that He didn't need them in heaven either.

I was not content to just be in God's presence. I wanted to be doing something for Him. He, on the other hand, desired a love relationship with me.

He reminded me that He didn't create man to work for Him. He created man for relationship.

He reminded me that He created the heavens and earth without man's help and He was capable of taking care of everything He created, including man.

He shared with me that He could do all the work that needed to be done alone, but that I was needed in our relationship.

Do you desire to *know* God intimately or are you content to have Him be a beneficent magistrate who gives you unmerited favor? Do you love God the Father with your ALL or do you just appreciate who He is and what He has done for you?

Do you need to be performing works to feel worthy or is God's presence in you your treasure? Is God's presence enough for you or will you check out of heaven?

Living grace is loving God our Father with our ALL—giving Him our life so that He can give us His LIFE. Grace is the path to knowing our Father and Jesus Christ whom He sent.

Final Thoughts on Grace

Grace is not just a attribute of God or an aspect of His character. Grace is another word for Christ—God manifested through man.

Interpreting grace as God's unmerited favor is to miss the purpose of God's grace and to miss one of the main themes of salvation. Living in grace is our salvation. Grace points us to our LIVING SAVIOR and LORD. Grace defines how we are to relate to our Father.

In reality GRACE has all to do with what choices we make.

If we choose to listen to God's voice and heed His promptings, we are saved. We believe in Him whom God our Father sent to show us the WAY.

If we choose not to heed His words or to follow His motivations in our heart, then we are refusing to believe.

A question to ask ourselves is this: *How would I conduct my life if I believed God's Spirit was in my heart and reigning?*

We say we have given our life to the LORD but our actions show we retain control of our lives. Jesus, however, did nothing but what God the Father said and did through Him.

Instead of following Jesus' example, we do what we think is the right thing to do and ask God to bless our undertakings. Well might it be said of us:

> *For the sake of your tradition, you have made void the word of God. You hypocrites! Well did Isaiah prophesy of you, when he said:* **'This people honors me with their lips, but their heart is far from me; in vain do they worship me***, teaching as doctrines the precepts of men.'*
> *Matthew 15:6-9*

We honor God with our lips but we don't give Him our hearts. We think we are worshiping God with our rituals and praises but He desires true worship.

> *I appeal to you therefore, brethren, by the mercies of God,* **to present your bodies as a living sacrifice***, holy and acceptable to God,* **which is your spiritual worship.** *Do not be conformed to this world but be transformed by the renewal of your mind, that you may prove what is the will of God, what is good and acceptable and perfect.*
> *Romans 12:1-2*

> *Jesus said to her, "Woman, believe me, the hour is coming when neither on this mountain nor in Jerusalem will you worship the Father...the hour is coming, and now is, when the true worshipers will* **worship the Father in spirit and truth, for such the Father seeks to worship him. God is spirit, and those who worship him must worship in spirit and truth.***"* *John 4: 21-24*

Grace is another word for faith—faith in a LIVING LORD and SAVIOR. Grace is all about a personal relationship with God our Father. This relationship is ours because of God's unmerited favor, but this grace must be received and lived.

Grace is not about who God is, it is about the relationship He has with us and the importance of this relationship in our salvation. *Grace is about God's presence in us and His expression through us.*

God designed us to have His Spirit within as our source of good. Jesus came to reconcile us to His original design—God in us.

Grace is God's divine influence upon our heart and His reflection in our life. Living in grace is glorifying our LORD. Refusing to live in grace is denying our LORD and the work of the cross.

My prayer for anyone reading this book is that you will seek to know God in this intimate way. I pray that you will seek to have the kingdom of God within you and allow God's Spirit to reign in your heart. I ask God to open your heart and soften it so that you can hear His tender voice from within and know what a wonderful gift our LORD has given us—His GRACE.

Appendix: Grace—An Epistle Greeting and Ending

One important aspect of grace that bears noting is the number of times the word grace appears in the greetings and endings of the epistles. Most of the epistles begin and end with a reference to grace. I have listed these verses here so that you can see the many references to grace.

My question is: Why is grace used and not love or faith, which are of utmost importance in our walk? Why do most of the writers of these epistles use grace to begin and end their letters?

I believe it is because grace encompasses all that pertains to our walk of faith. Grace is the essence of believing in Christ. It is the courage to walk as Jesus did in God's Spirit. Grace is loving God our Father with our whole being—giving Him our all.

Let's review then the greetings and endings of the New Testament epistles:

Romans

Romans 1:7 **Grace** *to you and* **peace** *from God our Father and the Lord Jesus Christ.*

Romans 16:20 *The* **grace** *of our Lord Jesus Christ be with you.*

1 Corinthians

1 Corinthians 1:3-4 **Grace** *to you and* **peace** *from God our Father and the Lord Jesus Christ. I give thanks to God always for you because of the* **grace** *of God which was given you in Christ Jesus.*

1 Corinthians 16:23 *The* **grace** *of the Lord Jesus be with you.*

2 Corinthians

2 Corinthians 1:2 **Grace** *to you and* **peace** *from God our Father and the Lord Jesus Christ.*

2 Corinthians 13:14 *The* **grace** *of the Lord Jesus Christ and the love of God and the fellowship of the Holy Spirit be with you all.*

Galatians

Galatians 1:3 **Grace** *to you and* **peace** *from God the Father and our Lord Jesus Christ,*

Galatians 6:18 *The* **grace** *of our Lord Jesus Christ* **be with your spirit**, *brethren. Amen.*

Ephesians

Ephesians 1:2 **Grace** *to you and* **peace** *from God our Father and the Lord Jesus Christ.*

Ephesians 6:24 **Grace** *be with all who love our Lord Jesus Christ with love undying.*

Philippians

Philippians 1:2 **Grace** *to you and* **peace** *from God our Father and the Lord Jesus Christ.*

Philippians 4:23 *The* **grace** *of the Lord Jesus Christ* **be with** *your spirit.*

Colossians

Colossians 1:2 **Grace** *to you and* **peace** *from God our Father.*

Colossians 4:18 *Grace be with you.*

1 Thessalonians

1 Thessalonians 1:1 *Grace to you and peace.*

1 Thessalonians 5:28 *The* **grace** *of our Lord Jesus Christ be with you.*

2 Thessalonians

2 Thessalonians 1:2 **Grace** *to you and* **peace** *from God the Father and the Lord Jesus Christ.*

2 Thessalonians 3:18 *The* **grace** *of our Lord Jesus Christ be with you all.*

1 Timothy

1 Timothy 1:2 **Grace**, *mercy, and* **peace** *from God the Father and Christ Jesus our Lord.*

1 Timothy 6:21 *Grace be with you.*

2 Timothy

2 Timothy 1:2 *Grace, mercy, and* **peace** *from God the Father and Christ Jesus our Lord.*

2 Timothy 4:22 *The Lord* **be with your spirit.** *Grace be with you.*

Titus

Titus 1:4 *Grace and* **peace** *from God the Father and Christ Jesus our Savior.*

Titus 3:15 *Grace be with you all.*

Philemon

Philemon 3 *Grace to you and* **peace** *from God our Father and the Lord Jesus Christ.*

Philemon 25 *The grace of the Lord Jesus Christ* **be with your spirit.**

James

*James*_____

*James*_____

Hebrews

*Hebrews*_____

Hebrews 13:25 *Grace be with all of you. Amen.*

1 Peter

1 Peter 1:2 *May* **grace** *and* **peace** *be multiplied to you.*

1 Peter 5:12 *I have written briefly to you, exhorting and declaring that this is the true* **grace** *of God;* **stand fast in it.**

2 Peter

2 Peter 1:2   May **grace** and **peace** be multiplied to you in the knowledge of God and of Jesus our Lord.

2 Peter 3:18   But **grow in the grace** and knowledge of our Lord and Savior Jesus Christ.

1 John

*1 John*_____

*1 John*_____

2 John

*2 John*_____

2 John 3   **Grace,** mercy, and **peace** will be with us, from God the Father and from Jesus Christ the Father's Son, in truth and love.

3 John

*3 John*_____

*3 John*_____

Jude

Jude_____

Jude_____

Revelations

Revelation 1:4   **Grace** to you and **peace** from him who is and who was and who is to come, and from the seven spirits who are before his throne,

Revelation 22:21   The **grace** of the Lord Jesus be with all the saints. Amen.

All the epistles except James, 1 & 3 John, and Jude contain the word grace in their greeting and/or closing. This I believe is significant. I believe that Peter, John, Paul and the other writers of these letters understood the importance of living in grace and included it as a reminder to believers to live in grace and not revert to the law.

When Peter ends his first epistle, he encourages believers to *stand fast in grace*. He is encouraging them to live in grace and not be disheartened and revert to the law. If grace is interpreted as God's unmerited favor, why would Peter be encouraging them to stand fast in God's unmerited favor?

When Peter ends his second epistle, he encourages them to *grow in grace*. I believe he is encouraging them to listen to God's voice and heed His promptings from God's Spirit within them. If grace is interpreted as God's unmerited favor, how does one grow in God's unmerited favor?

The writers of these letters are encouraging believers to live in grace—God's divine influence upon their heart and God's expression in their life.

Grace is not mentioned in the gospels except for one reference to Jesus who demonstrated God's grace for us.

> *And **the Word became flesh** and dwelt among us, **full of grace** and truth; we have beheld his glory, glory as of the only Son from the Father.... **And from his fulness have we all received, grace upon grace**. For the law was given through Moses; **grace** and truth **came through Jesus Christ**.*   *John 1:14-17*

Grace became available to us only after Christ won our reconciliation with God our Father.

> *Now this he said about the Spirit, which those who believed in him were to receive; for as yet the Spirit had*

not been given, because Jesus was not yet glorified.
John 7:39

*The Counselor, the **Holy Spirit,** whom the Father will send in my name, he **will teach you all things, and bring to your remembrance all that I have said to you.** Peace I leave with you; my peace I give to you; not as the world gives do I give to you. Let not your **hearts** be troubled, neither let them be afraid.* John 14:26-27

Notice the word *peace* here and where I have highlighted it as part of the greetings and closings above. Use of this word *peace* along with grace is not accidental.

According to Strong's Greek Concordance *peace* means "to set at one again."

> 1515. eirēnē eirene; probably from a primary verb eirō eiro **(to join)**; peace (literally or figuratively); by implication, prosperity:—**one**, peace, quietness, **rest, set at one again**.

By using the word *peace* the writers acknowledge our return to oneness with our Father that Jesus won for us. They acknowledge God's initial design of a oneness relationship with Him. We are *set at one again* with our Father God as it was in the Garden of Eden before man separated himself from God.

Peace comes when we return to His original design and purpose for creating us. Peace is ours when we live in grace—in oneness with God's Spirit and allow His influence upon our heart and His expression in our life.

***Grace** to you and **peace** from God the Father and the Lord Jesus Christ.*

For by grace
[*God's Spirit—Christ—expressed in and through you*]
you have been saved
[*each and every moment*]
through faith
[*in His presence in you*];
and this
[*your salvation and healing*]
is not your own doing,
it is the gift of God
[*His presence in you*]
— not because of [*your own*] *works,*
lest any man should boast.
For we are his workmanship,
created in Christ Jesus for [*God's*] *good works,*
which God prepared beforehand,
that we should walk in them
[*God's works done in and through us when we submit and follow His leading from within*].
Ephesians 2:8-10

About the Author

Carolyn Bardsley studied Scripture for most of her adult life. Over time she realized she had considerable head knowledge but little heart connection to her Lord. This troubled her when she read Jesus' rebuke of the Pharisees for their knowledge of Scripture, yet refusing to come to Him—a LIVING SAVIOR. She was also troubled by the commandment to love the Lord because how could she love someone without having her heart engaged? Having been taught to distrust her heart, this dilemma caused her to study what Scripture said about the heart and mind which revealed the importance of *believing in our heart*.

In the 1980s Carolyn developed and taught a gifts and calling workshop for churches. Since Carolyn had developed and taught career and life planning workshops in corporations, she had a unique perspective on how spiritual gifts relate to motivations and skills in jobs and careers. In these workshops she saw how many people were disconnected from their hearts. She could identify with them having lived in her mind for most of her life.

In the 1990s Carolyn realized that God wants to talk with people today. While studying Scripture about hearing God, she was surprised to find that hearing God's voice was a function of the heart. *"Today, when you hear his voice do not harden your hearts." "Believe in your heart."* Knowing that as a believer she had the Spirit of the LIVING GOD in her heart, she began to trust that God would speak to her if she trusted in His presence in her. Daily quiet time became a conversation with the Lord. Scripture became a pointer to a LIVING LORD and SAVIOR—

not just a biography about Him. Her faith became one of believing in her heart because God's Spirit resides there.

During a time of illness she sought to understand how God provided comfort during suffering. The Scripture *"My grace is sufficient for you, for my strength is made perfect in weakness,"* prompted her to look up what grace meant. Grace as "God's unmerited favor" did not console her. Her grace study, using Scripture and *Strong's Greek Concordance*, dramatically changed her understanding of grace. She writes about her new understanding of grace in her books *Grace* and *Living In Grace*.

Her discovery about the importance of heart faith and living in grace has been so profound in her own walk of faith that she joys to share it with others to strengthen their faith in a LIVING LORD AND SAVIOR who seek to have a heart relationship with them.

Made in United States
North Haven, CT
26 February 2024

49241142R00118